wisdom:
what I wish
I had known

Wisdom: What I wish I had known
Copyright © Kiwwih September 2009

Standard Edition ISBN 978-0-9563363-0-9

Second Edition September 2009

Printed and bound in Great Britain by Direct Print On Demand Ltd
Designed by Resource Management Design
Printed on FSC approved paper.
Published by Kiwwih

contents:

mission statement:

> We hope to empower young people
> such as ourselves to give them
> the best life tool possible; Wisdom.

foreword:

It is a privilege to be asked to write this foreword. Matthew and his team have, in the production of this book, shown that they know far more at 18 than I ever did: not just in terms of business acumen but also in terms of teamwork, dedication and persistence. As you will see, the array of contributors is impressive, from all walks of life. As one would expect, therefore, the advice this book contains is varied, instructive and pertinent . . . and not a little entertaining in places too!

True education is about far more than exam results, about far more than placing young people on the stereotyped treadmill to middle-class success. I hope schools teach that and school leavers know that. If the variety of experiences this book contains reinforces that lesson, it will have achieved its aim. If it inspires some to success, it will have achieved its aim. If it entertains and instructs, it will have achieved its aim. I suspect it will do all three.

Can I add my thanks to those of Matthew and his team to all those who have contributed: I hope they are pleased with the product. And can I add my thanks – not without a little pride as their Head Master – to the A21 Young Enterprise Business that made this book happen.

John Moule
Head Master
Bedford School

introduction:

This book was originally conceived by a21, a group of Year 12 students from Bedford School who embarked on the Young Enterprise Programme in September 2008. The group was looking to produce a unique product that would set them apart from their peers. After much deliberation they decided to take on the ambitious task of producing a book that combined the knowledge from various inspirational people, from various occupations. The book was a representation of the commitment, the team spirit and the motivation the team possessed to produce such a wealth of wisdom. The business has now progressed from Young Enterprise. Matthew Ayres still leads the business team and has rebranded it Kiwwih. With profits being donated to the Prince's Trust.

Producing this book has been at times enjoyable, stressful and even painful, but most importantly it resulted in being incredibly rewarding and an education in itself. Together we have learnt much about how businesses and people work, which is something we would not have achieved within the classroom. Throughout this process we have had our low points, but our moments of great joy also as we finally realised our dream; to produce a commercially viable book.

This book is not an academic work and should not be read as a text book. It is rather a collection of life stories which brings to the reader the most important, perhaps most priceless of commodities – wisdom. It is not simply a book which tells you about different careers, but also about personal experiences and life lessons. Through this book, we aim to inspire and motivate people of all ages.

Wisdom is invaluable in life and some of the greatest lessons we learn come from the advice of our elders. Education is something that can be gained through teaching in a classroom, whereas wisdom comes from experience. Many people believe that the only way to learn is by learning from our mistakes. However, why should we do this when it is much more productive to learn from both the mistakes and successes of other people?

There are two ways to gain wisdom: either you encounter each of your own mistakes and learn from them, or you seek counsel from those who have come before and learn from their mistakes and successes. As the well known proverb says:

> " A wise man learns by the experience of others;
> a fool, by his own. "

" You do better at stuff you enjoy "

Sir Nicholas Grimshaw

Architecture

Architecture

Architecture involves the design and construction of buildings and other physical structures. Architects transform creative ideas into reality by organising space, mass, form, volume, texture, structure, and materials.

A creative flair combined with an ability to transfer your ideas onto paper through drawings and sketches is important, as well as the ability to understand people's needs and how to provide for them. Design influences everyone, every minute of the day. We take for granted much of what has been designed around us. Architects sometimes extend their design skills to products as well as to buildings. It is also important to note that architecture is not all about the exterior appearance of the building. There is a huge amount of detailing which goes into the creation of a building, from the selection of exterior construction materials down to the specifications of internal fixtures and fittings.

All architects must be registered and obtain a licence from the Architects Registration Board to operate within the UK. This is because you will have to take into account legislation concerning Health & Safety and Building Regulations as well as the requirements of the occupants when designing structures.

SIR NICHOLAS GRIMSHAW

Architect

Profession/short job description:
I find it hard to describe exactly what an architect does. To be an architect in today's world you need to be able to handle public relations, accountants, business, law and the environment. I find it interesting from an A Level point of view that people are encouraged to do a narrow spectrum. But people need to have a broad subject choice as well, as Architecture is so much more than buildings and drawings. Even more so now with the environment; green elements are now starting to shape architecture. Buildings are going to develop differently. Styles of architecture will instead be driven by the environment, as opposed to the current style clashes which go on today. It would be a very innovative time to start architecture, so take advantage of this.

Finding out what architecture is about is not easy. It is very difficult to do; visiting an architecture practice is a good start and I strongly encourage that. I personally got into architecture through going to an architects practice. Finding what you want to do in life is very difficult, you need to have some sort of inkling if you want to do something.

How did you make your first steps to success, and what do you consider to be the key to your success?
I was lucky; I had an uncle who was involved in bringing students from Africa to find work in England. My uncle had a row of houses which needed refurbishment and he thought I could handle the job.

Grimshaw chose housing ideas and developed our own entrepreneurial housing scheme. Our big break was a block of flats so this will always be a major moment for me.

To be successful as an architect you need to be able to fight your own battles; it is a competitive world. Both universities and firms are looking for people with bright sparks. They are looking for diversity and brightness, which accounts for a lot in architecture. Be entrepreneurial and create your own opportunities to get ahead in a diverse and varied profession.

What have been your most valuable career-defining experiences?
I suppose it was the co-initiative house scheme; designing a building and then living in it for six years was very interesting. Talking to other residents was good because it opened my eyes to their lives and how they wanted to live.

My second defining experience would be learning how to take a grilling in a tough interview. The toughness of getting interviews for a job against other firms. The idea of trying to develop a relationship with someone on the other side of the table is crucial. People have got to be able to like you to work with you. It is make or break and goes on constantly within architecture. You have to be able to engage with them and listen. Do not impose ideas on people. People are responsive to listeners.

Thirdly, the absolute excitement of a national project. Like our Waterloo Station project in London, which every practice in the country wanted. It is great to know that millions of people will be using a building which you designed.

What do you wish you had known when you were younger?
Well I suppose I would have benefited enormously from people talking to me about the possibilities of life. At school life is organised around subjects, which do not always have much bearing with the real world. I think it would have helped a great deal to have something to look at and see; visiting places and work experience.

The gap year is a wonderful opportunity and it works well and provides huge advantages to people. I am very lucky having ended up in architecture; my brother taught at Edinburgh University and he showed me around and I took an interest in art and design. You do better at stuff you enjoy.

Do you have a personal Mantra?

Nothing gets done by imposing stuff on people. If I can not get my message across, if people do not feel supportive, nobody gets anywhere.

So my mantra is "take people with you".

Obama is a great example of this, because he believes so much he takes others with him. You can be a bully all your life and get nowhere.

Are there any funny / comic moments that you can remember from your career?

Architecture is a serious business. We do enjoy ourselves though, but nothing of notable comic worth - such as falling flat on my face in wet concrete.

What advice would you have for young people just starting out in the world?

Do not feel pressurised. In many ways you are made to do something and feel that change is impossible. On the contrary you have choices, life is flexible. The problem today is that people are very good at filling in boxes and impressing. So it is hard to find those special people who have that ability.

Be enthusiastic about life - as being pressurised makes you close avenues, as opposed to opening things up. Architecture is so diverse so have a wide range of interests. You could be interested in the environment and social issues, but be rubbish at drawings. It really does not matter. It is the concept that counts. Be open. Don't try to be perfect, keep an open mind, keep asking questions.

Is there anything else that you would like to add?

I want to end on a note of enthusiasm.

The world of architecture combined with the environment and new world planning is a great new opportunity. Whatever your abilities there are so many different jobs out there. The age in which we live is exciting and will continue to be so.

I would encourage all to look at the environment area; a lot of professions interlock in that area. The environmental field overarches into all areas not just architecture.

PROF. KARL-HEINZ PETZINKA

Architect

As top-of-the-year student at the University of Aachen I began to work for one of the most famous architects and theoreticians, Oswald Mathias Ungers in Cologne; after having received no reply from any of my 90 applications. I had the determination to work there, which I had always dreamed of.

Courage, ambition, discipline and most importantly enjoyment at work always motivated me to the maximum. I was not on a great salary, but I learned to work for the architecture rather than for money. I got better through the work I did and my boss gave me the ability to learn a lot of things because I was highly motivated. In the end I earned so much more in terms of skill, that I forgot about how much I was paid. First of all, the work and effort, then the return.

To do everything as well as one can and to take on challenges willingly as well as to be a friend towards other people and to hold values of life high in regard, are the keys for life and also for success. And while I have always recognised the chance which opened up for me., there were always promoters involved as well: my professor Wolfgang Döring and Mathias Ungers opened up many opportunities and chances for me. Thus, they supported me at any time. I have learned that openness and engagement in everything I did was the reason why my mentors supported me. They have profited from it and I pass on exactly the same idea to my students and to people in my surroundings. I am very happy to pass onto others everything that I have experienced.

Just once did I hesitate to take on a new challenge. I was asked to be in charge of the expansion of the airport in Frankfurt to become the most important centre of Europe. The Prime-minister of Hessen, Koch, as chairman of the supervisory board, urged me to take it on. However, a feeling inside me did not let me say 'yes' and I ultimately followed this instinct. The woman who was appointed instead was fired after one year as managing director for the same task I was meant to do. She was made responsible for a major problem at the airport of Manila, although it was not her fault. After all, my instinct was right.

When I was younger, I wish I had known that sometimes ambition does not always lead to the right decision: one's instincts are also very important. The difficulty of knowing everything at the right time stayed, but the estimation of chances and issues got better due to my own experiences. I wish I had recognised this earlier, but it will never change and in the end this knowledge is called 'wisdom'.

Do what you do, as well as you can. Such success will get you to the maximum. First and foremost, always pay attention to everything around you. Show respect towards your fellow men and to allow openness in oneself. Accept help and support and to be ready at any time, to pass on this experience to others. "Please" and "Thank you" are no disgrace.

Your family, friends and your surroundings will keep you grounded and will give you self-confidence. Self-confidence also means believing in the good, even if life is very often difficult. In the end you should be sure and should know that the life you lived had a purpose. Very often, you pay society a certain amount back of what you gained and this is nothing to be scared of. To be able to give is much more important than to accept gifts.

Very happily I pass on to you my congratulations and how fantastic I find this project. I would have loved, to be able to take on such a challenge with my friends in my school-days. I am very proud of all who have taken part. I am also just as proud of the teachers who taught you to take on challenges. It is your time – you have to show what you are capable of. You have to show us, how you want to accept your world in order to be able to pass on a good foundation.

BOONMA YONGPRAKIT

Architect

Professional / Short Job Description
I am an Architect.

How did you make the first steps to success, and what do you consider to be the key to your success?
I wanted to be an architect ever since I was child. I enjoy building and drawing. I like my job because I get to travel to many places around the world to design and work on my projects. I don't really consider myself a successful person. I just love and like what I do; so in that sense it enables me to be successful.

I am still working on my dream to have my own design studio.

To answer your questions about the key to success, I think you have to work hard and love what you are doing no matter what you do just focus and telling to yourself that there is nothing that you can't do. Some day you will be happy and successful in your career.

What do you wish you had known when you were younger?
When I was a small child, I wish I had known more about the world. I could have done better if I had had better advice from my teacher. I learned a lot on my own from the environment which surrounded me. That might be the reason why I wanted to be an architect because my uncle and brother were builders.

Do you have a personal mantra?
Focus and try to do your best.

What advice would you have for young people just starting out in the world?
First of all you have to ask yourself what you would like to do and find out how to get there. You will be the happiest person in the world if you like what you are doing. So listening to yourself is the key and make it work.

Is there anything else you would like to add?
Please think positively and that will give you a base as a happy person.

> Celebrate Mistakes. You can always learn much more from your mistakes than your successes

James Dyson

Business

Business

Business is the core of world economic stability, affecting our lives on a day to day basis. Those directly employed in the business world often fall under three sectors; those who run their own businesses, company shareholders, and company employees. Businesses can encapsulate every single one of the world's markets, from selling food and drink, to producing high tech communications technology. Within business you could be involved in management, sales, marketing, technology, human resources to name but a few.

Ultimately business is about making profit and in order to start up your own business all you need is an idea and determination. Business skills are often innate and many people have a natural instinct when it comes to spotting a niche in the market, the essence of all successful business ventures. On the other hand, you can improve your business acumen by selecting a Business course at University where most courses cover marketing, productions, management techniques and touch upon accounting and finance.

EMMA AYRES

Managing Director of The Bennie Group Ltd

The Bennie Group is a family run group of companies based in Burton Latimer, Kettering. It employs nearly 300 people and turns over £25 million pounds a year.

I could start by telling you what I do as a job and run through from an early age as to how I got to be here, but I'm more than a little concerned that my children will use it as an obituary when I die so I'll turn it on its head and write about what I can remember of being 18 and what would've been useful to know then.

At the age of 18 I was actually still at school. My parents had decided when I was 16 that I was competent enough to follow my father to Oxford and a learned education. My school at that time was headed up by a formidable Ms. Trunchball type, who, under the newly acquired state school status, had no desire to put any candidates forward for Oxbridge. So I found myself transferred to a local private school, formerly (by one year) all boys, and as the examining boards were different I had to re-do my Lower 6th year. Moving from an all girls school to a mixed system and prolonging the agony of attending school by another year, together with the freedom of being able to drive (when not grounded) all helped to demolish any plans that my venerable parents may have had about Oxford. I eventually managed to achieve 3 unremarkable grades at A level, was offered University places outside of Oxbridge, but spurned the notion of any further academic learning and instead embarked with great vigour on life (and business).

I had never grown up expecting to go into the family business simply because I was not male; and it was, and still is, a very male dominated business. When I announced to my father that I was going for a job interview he was offended that I hadn't even considered the family business and suggested I give it a go. I would have to start at the bottom, naturally, as I had nothing to offer, no skill or trade! Having worked in the school holidays and on most Saturdays cleaning the toilets I thought it could only get better... and so started my career at The Bennie Group. It's not for the faint hearted, I can assure you. I was full of life, exuberance, enthusiasm and drive. If I kept my nose clean, learnt the business and followed my father's ethos, it was going to be simple! I liked a challenge that didn't come out of a text book! This challenge was going to be great fun.
To set the scene - we are talking about the Construction industry in the early 1980's, and I mean the heavy duty end of the industry; quarrying (that's excavators and rock-blasting), bulk earthmoving (that's diggers, blades, shovels and articulated dump-trucks), oil distribution (tankers), heavy haulage (more than 6 axles, big enough to move centurion tanks for the army), fork lift truck hire and the odd one out for a construction group, a company that manufactures orthopaedic shoes.
In a workforce where less than 5% of the employees are female and being the boss's daughter I had to toughen up very quickly. It was hard work earning the respect of my colleagues, and I consider it to have been doubly hard to overcome the scepticism of being female and having a birthright. But I just put my head down and worked harder at it, and I was all the more determined not to waste the opportunity.

The odds were stacked against me when I was tasked with running the tipper desk at the age of 21, in charge of over 30 drivers. What did I know about what a lorry driver could and couldn't do, and how could I ask them to do a job that I couldn't do myself? There was only one answer, and it seemed very exciting, so I went off and got my HGV licence. Actually I hold an HGV 1. Naively, when I turned up for the training and was asked whether I was going for my class 1 (artics) or a class 2 (rigid vehicles), I replied that I thought the class category was determined by how well you drove!
25 years later, and following the sudden death of my father, I found myself running the family business, single-handed, isolated and now totally alone. Not only had I lost my father, I'd also lost my mentor, a man who I greatly admired and whose achievements in life and business I was in awe of. Turning over £25 million and employing nearly 300 people is my way of life because I have grown up with it; it's not daunting, but it can be frustrating. In the construction industry the female boss is viewed more with novelty than taken seriously, and men in general (there are always exceptions to any rule) find it difficult to work for a woman and find it even more difficult to accept criticism from a woman. For all its frustrations, I'm passionate about making a success of it and I look forward to the challenges that each day brings.

On reflection it would have been useful to have worked somewhere other than in the family business, at least for a few years, to give me a broader outlook. I was offered a job at a Caterpillar distributorship in Marketing (my one and only job interview), but turned it down because it did not offer enough excitement as a job. I was also selected by Cranfield University to do a part-time MBA course, but turned them down because they were targeting women as opposed to being selected on merit (pride can come before a fall). I've regretted this since and I have spent much time subsequently at Cranfield on various business based courses and believe that my earlier perception that it would be too academic and too institutionalised was ill-founded.

- Believe in yourself and have confidence in your own abilities
- Follow your strengths and learn from your weaknesses
- People, especially friends, are the most important thing in life and the old adage that you can count your real friends on the fingers of one hand is absolutely true
- Train yourself to remember people's names and one or two key facts about them. They'll be flattered that you remember them and they won't forget you!
- Be approachable, be honest to yourself and remember that you have to earn respect
- You are never too old to learn something new
- When faced with an insurmountable problem and contemplating how to handle it, remember how you would eat an elephant – in bite sized chunks!
- Be passionate about what you do; learn your business inside out and know how it all fits together
- In business it's important to recognise the foot soldiers; you would not exist without them
- Learn to talent spot people on their way up in life; they are the leaders of tomorrow
- Get yourself a mentor
- Being a woman in a 'mans' world can open doors that would otherwise be difficult, but use this skill wisely
- Your business is only as good as the people in it. Loyalty is important, and like trust, it's a two way street.

To sum everything up, education, hard work, commitment and dedication are all very necessary for success, but don't forget to have some fun whilst you are developing your business skills or all too late you will realise that life has passed you by and something called the recession comes along, kicks you in the teeth for no apparent reason and demands a doubling of your efforts to merely slow down your company's backward steps. Make sure you have the energy to meet it head on and win. Good luck, your life can be what you want it to be. Just dare to dream!

www.thebenniegroup.co.uk

DAVID BARLOW

Field Sales Manager, Brembo UK

Brief Job Description:
I report directly to Brembo, Italy, responsible for the development and growth of both the Brembo and Bradi brands within the whole of the IFA group, here in the UK, together with our account in Southern Ireland. Responsible for negotiations with Italy for all pricing, marketing, promotions, administration, technical support and sales growth, so as to meet the set goals and standards required by Brembo International. Also working in close liaison with the UK logistics centre in Kidderminster and the financial centre in Bristol so as to ensure smooth and continuous operation and supply of product.

My First Steps to Success:
Probably my first step to success was, as with most people, in the most part luck and being in the right place at the right time. For a time I served as a qualified engineer and draughtsman my thoughts of a future career had never been in the 'selling' sphere yet I was constantly told by a secretary of mine, when I was Chief Draughtsman, that I really should go into selling as I had "the gift of the gab".

I had at the time just met my 'wife to be' and decided that a new venture may not be a bad idea and anyway, I really had nothing to lose as I could always go back into engineering, jobs were plentiful back in those days, the 1970's. To cut a long story short, I applied for three sales jobs; one was selling fire extinguishers, one selling newspaper advertising space and the other selling industrial construction diamond products and machinery. The first I didn't get but was offered a position with the two others. As the latter was more mechanically minded I decided to go for that and am pleased to report that I have never looked back.

It was as though this was my true vocation, it was almost like the 'Midas touch' where everything just seemed to slot into place and after a few short weeks, three to be exact, orders started flooding in and within a year turned an area from £20,000 per anum to £200,000 per anum. This was my first steps to success and quite simply they key was, and still is, work hard, be totally honest with your customer and yourself, be prepared to make mistakes but be quick to correct them, accept there will always be difficult days but 'tomorrow is another day' and most importantly 'be yourself'.

Most Valuable Career Defining Moment:
There are probably three that have clearly defined my future. The first was when I was a 20 year old apprentice. I was asked to go and do some mundane work in the drawing office, doing very long mathematical calculations (remember computers were not about in the late 60's) and during this week or so the Chief Draughtsman commented on my neat printing and asked would I be interested in working as an engineering draughtsman. This was my dream job from my school days but unfortunately due to the fact that I came from a poor and large family in Lancashire both myself and my twin brother were not allowed to stay on at school for the necessary exams that I needed to apply for a draughtsmanship and had to take almost any job that paid a wage. Considering that when I started my six year mechanical engineering apprenticeship at 15, my wage was £3 - 5 shillings per week, but we were all grateful that some extra money was coming in to the family pot. From this lucky break of starting work in a drawing office I then studied for another 6 years and qualified as an Engineering Design Draughtsman.

The second was meeting my wife when at the age of 29, in October 1978; we got married and never looked back. There is the comment that "behind every good man, there is a good woman". This was and still is without doubt the best and strongest statement ever made.

The third was when, just 3 years ago this January, my 21 year old daughter was diagnosed with Leukaemia, completely out of the blue. This was truly a terrifying period of my life as we came very close to losing her, but I am pleased to report that after a 6 month stay in hospital she has gone from strength to strength, nursing on the ward where she was cared for and will be going to university in September studying to be a Staff Nurse. We never presume all is ok, she has to have bone-marrow extractions every 4 months but as each day goes by we are getting nearer to that 6 year 'all clear' deadline. As a penultimate accolade to my engineering and sales career I had my name published in the 'Engineers Blue Book' along with the designatory letters after my name of T.Eng; MIET; MIED; S.Eng; Finst.SMM, for me a honour.

What do I wish I had known when I was younger?

Probably how to treat women better, but saying that I am still learning at the tender age of 59 and will probably never really know.

On a serious note, I would have to say nothing, life is a learning curve. I remember an old colleague of mine, who is no longer with us, telling me that the day you stop learning is the day you are, in his words, "pushing up daises". It's all down to experience, don't grow old too quickly, enjoy your youth and of course, enjoy life in general. We only have one crack at it so make the most of it.

Do I have a personal Mantra?

Yes, I probably do, my wife but have never thought too deeply in this manner and would not really want her to know this!!!!

Are there any funny moments in my career:

Absolutely yes, way too many to mention and way too many to actually tell anyone about due to precarious situations!

One or two I can mention is that I was once demonstrating a diamond chain saw used for cutting out the mortar between bricks for inserting a damp-course membrane. This particular job was on a very old and very expensive listed building in the beautiful Cheshire countryside. As I was making my cut along the mortar seam I forgot to stop and pack the gap with slate. Unfortunately to my horror the cut seam became too long and a 3 or 4 metre length of gable end of the property dropped around 15mm. I was very quickly told to pack my gear and leave (but using slightly stronger language). Couldn't get away too quickly as I had pulled my back doing the damn job!

Another one was when I was working as Chief Draughtsman. The factory employed only women on the shop floor and I was asked to make a study of a particular machine where the girls were working. Bearing in mind that it was the day we finished for Christmas holidays, I duly made my visit only to be faced with a screaming mob of females, ready to rape, abuse or even castrate anything in trousers. I made a very hasty retreat to my office, locked the door, hid behind my drawing board and waited until they retreated and relocated to the pub next to the factory for more refreshments. At the time it was terrifying but now I look back and think 'if only!'

Advice for young people

My advise is truly work hard, be kind to people and be totally honest with your life and be truthful to yourself.

If you fail first time, don't give up because you never know what is around the corner.

If you feel a cold coming on, go to work and 'sweat it off', you will feel far better for it than lying in bed and feeling sorry for yourself.

Enjoy life to the full and remember, every time you wake-up it's a new day for your new life. Things can sometimes look crap but remember there is always someone worse off than you and remember to smile, it's the best medicine ever.

Finally

Set your goals high, both in business and pleasure.

At school I was absolutely rubbish at sport but in my mid 40's started long distance running and successfully completed numerous marathons and road races throughout the UK.

As a boy, I longed to be a military drummer. Then purely by luck in my late 40's I started, and now have the pleasure of playing not only throughout the UK but in various parts of Europe as a lead drummer with The Yorkshire Volunteers Military Band and have even had the honour of playing at the 'Royal Tournament'.

REMEMBER NEVER GIVE UP –THE WORD IMPOSSIBLE DOES NOT EXIST.

AND LASTLY – GET YOURSELF A GOOD WOMAN !!!!

KARREN BRADY

Birmingham City Football Club Managing Director

The thing that I wish I knew when I was young was the importance of surrounding yourself with a good team. Of course individuals should themselves be driven, hard working and passionate about whatever they choose to do, but having a dedicated and committed team is hugely important too. It is definitely one of the keys to success.

PHIL BROWN

CEO of Causeway Technologies Ltd

Profession/short job description:
Chief Executive of Causeway software company (£16m Revenue, EBITDA £4m, 180 employees).

How did you make your first steps to success, and what do you consider to be the key to your success?
My first steps to success were taken when at the age of 23, I decided to leave my comfortable job and try my luck in London working in sales for an IT company. Until that point I had completed a BSc degree in Building Technology and duly entered the Construction Industry. I soon learned the vast difference between a job with cosy salary and a company car and a job in an aggressive entrepreneurial environment where you only earned money if you sold things.

What have been your most valuable career-defining experiences?
Deciding at the age of 24 to start up my first business - I had realised by then that as a young man I had everything to gain and little to lose so I threw myself into it full of determination and belief.

What do you wish you had known when you were younger?
That it's all about hiring the best people you can afford and empowering them - in the early days I thought I could do it all myself.

Do you have a personal Mantra?
Follow your instincts but always think things through, make the tough decisions that need to be made and then execute with conviction.

Are there any funny / comic moments that you can remember from your career?
One of the funniest moments was in the very early days when a prospective customer wanted to carry out a customer reference visit. Before placing an order with us for our software, the prospect wanted to talk to any existing customers that were already using our newly developed Purchase Order Management (POM) system - the only problem was that we had only a handful of customers at that stage and none of them were using the new POM system. If you've ever seen the movie 'Sting', then you'll work out what our solution to this conundrum was. We managed to convince our tamest customer to allow one of our employees to pretend to be his Buyer and to host the prospective customer's reference visit. So the day came and our employee headed over to our customer's offices and was sat behind the Buyer's desk and became John the Buyer for the day. I arrived with the prospect and all was going well until the Buyer from the prospect started asking John what price he was paying for various building materials. John obviously knew how to demonstrate the POM system, but he hadn't a clue about the price of Bricks or Concrete! So, in a panic he excused himself from the meeting saying he needed to make a quick phone call. Unbeknown to me at that time was that he had ran downstairs, got in his car and drove off leaving the tame customer, the prospective customer and myself all sitting in silence wondering what was happening. After 10 minutes had passed I went out into the open office and asked a secretary did she know where John had gone, to which she replied (in full earshot of the prospect) "Who is John?".
Mortifying.
I still got the order though.

What advice would you have for young people just starting out in the world of business?
You'll only find your limitations when you abandon your comfort zone so believe in yourself, and start young when you're less fearful and the risk of failure isn't so costly.

Is there anything else that you would like to add?
Work as hard as you can, hold yourself and others accountable and most of all show humility.

www.causeway.com

ANDY BUTTFIELD

Director of a Motor Parts Wholesaler & Chairman
of the Independent Motor Factors Association

I left school without any academic qualification at the age of fifteen. My first Job was as an Apprentice Motor Mechanic and probably with very little real ambition other than getting away from school. At this time my only drive was an ability to learn quickly and a wish to find better ways of doing things. As with most teenagers, my attentions for the first few years after leaving school were filled with visits to the pub and the attractions of the opposite sex. I did manage to obtain some trade qualifications but soon began to realise I was becoming bored with the career I had chosen and began to look for something else. I tried a couple of non motor trade management jobs which did not really fill the role, along with becoming married and soon having a family, made me look back to the trade I started out in.

Almost by mistake I took a job as an Assistant Manager of a Motor Factor and it wasn't too long before I realised that this may just be an opportunity for me to progress. Fortunately, the job I had found was for a company that offered some training and the Managing Director was a driven and successful person. I progressed and on reflection a bit too quickly with this company, managing my own branch at the age of twenty two. The trouble with success to soon is you feel you should be offered the next step up the ladder immediately which of cause doesn't happen. This led me to a couple of changes which didn't really work out putting me back to square one.

I then found a job with my present company, although I didn't realise it at the time, I had the opportunity to start at the early stages of a new business set up by an extremely driven man who had enjoyed success with a national company and wanted to have the same success from his own business. Earlier experiences I had gained gave me the confidence to argue my point of view, that along with a memory for detail and the earlier mentioned wish to find a better way to do things must have made us a matching combination. I say this because we have worked together now for 31 years building the business from one small branch to 32 branches.

Would I have done anything different if I knew then what I know now?
I would probably have not done anything too different. Often your career is driven by your personal circumstances and in my case I had a young family and mortgage to support and present experiences wouldn't have changed the need to support them.

How do you measure success?
There is a balance between wealth, happiness and personal achievement. Wealth can often show others how well you have done. Happiness and personal achievement is what makes you feel that you've succeeded.

What advice would I give to someone starting out?
Listen and learn, make decisions, don't be frightened to change a wrong decision. Be sure you can afford the decisions you make, always look to find ways to improve, believe in your own abilities and work to them. The one person you shouldn't fool is yourself and lastly, always work 10% better and try harder than anyone else and you'll win.

ROD CALVERT OBE

Managing Director Millbrook Proving Ground
Ltd, Director GME Proving Grounds

My Current job is to manage Millbrook Proving Ground Ltd on a day to day basis. Millbrook provides automotive test, development and demonstration to the global automotive and component supplier industry.

My European roll involves directing activities at proving grounds in Germany and a cold weather development centre near the Arctic Circle in Sweden and my Global Roll involves coordinating the activities of General Motors Proving Grounds (similar to Millbrook) located around the world with facilities in; USA (2), Mexico, Canada, Brazil, Australia, Korea, China plus the European ones under direct management.

Millbrook as a legal entity and business with a profit and loss account and statutory accounts, has a marketing department, finance department handling invoicing, accounts receivable, payables, cash and tax, a production unit (manufacture of police cars and lpg vehicles around 2500 units per year), an Events and conferencing business, a venue for filming such as 5Th Gear and the Aston Martin crash scene in Casino Royale, the main engineering business which involves world class laboratories for powertrain and emissions research, a crash test laboratory performing among other things as Euro NCAP rating, tracks for evaluating all types of vehicles from motor cycles to heavy duty trucks and military vehicles.

General management of such a diverse Company involves leading a senior management team or Board. Each member having a specialisation, such as chief engineer, human resources, finance, marketing, operations, and facility maintenance. This Board meets weekly to review business issues and provide direction. Millbrook has a turn over of around £30m and around 400 staff.

Career steps to personal success in business
A good education with a thorough understanding of basic principles in chosen subjects

I had a technical education with an apprenticeship element where I learned and benefit to this day from all wood and metal working skills, a university degree in mechanical engineering and a masters degree in automotive engineering.

I worked in the steel industry in Sheffield but started my automotive career as a graduate engineer in the experimental department of Vauxhall Motors (and Bedford Trucks). After a number of years of training and two years assignment in the USA, I moved to the newly opened proving Ground at Millbrook. I worked hard to do the best job I could and soon was promoted through various roles and had the benefit of being involved in every discipline of the operation. I had further global experience within the GM global enterprise and in 1986 was manager of the facility, still at this stage a department of Vauxhall Motors/Bedford Trucks Product Engineering. In 1988 the legal entity Millbrook Proving Ground Ltd was formed and the company started trading and attempting to generate business from the global automotive and transport related industry. Millbrook has enjoyed cash generation and profitability consistently throughout its existence since 1988.

Success was recently endorsed by the award of an OBE 'for services to the automotive industry'

The key to personal success:
- Sound fundamental education; understand the basic principles do not just be an examination 'parrot'
- Once in your chosen profession accept any job, ask for more and be sure to do it well.
- Establish a reputation for integrity and delivering on time.
- Communicate, this is a two way process, learn to listen and be sure to say what you think and what you want. Remember, you have two ears and one mouth and as a young inexperienced person you will be surrounded by wisdom from all levels of the organisation, learn from it.
- Be confident in your own ability

Career defining moments
Negotiating my first big contract and realising that the supplier can have terms and conditions of supply not just

agreeing to accept the purchaser's terms.

Being totally alone in Detroit as a young untraveled, inexperienced engineer on the day Martin Luther-King was murdered and race riots started in the streets. Not having a hotel, mobile phone or any contacts. This was isolation in the scariest environment, a life defining experience.

As a junior and inexperienced manager, facing a union representative, who said, 'My members and I refuse to do the work you have asked us to do and what are you going to do about it?!' Everyone downed tools and sat on their work benches. What to do next? This was a career defining moment.

A major career defining moment was the day in 1988 when Millbrook was sold to Lotus Cars and I changed from being a departmental manager focussing mainly on technical job delivery to that of a business principal.

Business imperatives

There a three basic essentials to a successful business
The most important person is the customer
- Profit and return on investment must always be positive
- Cash is king and cash flow must be managed

There are many sub sets which lead to the essentials but without any one of the above a business will fail!

The key to developing the essentials is employee enthusiasm and engagement, achieved by communication, communication, communication!.
Businesses of every persuasion must deliver:
- Quality product
- On time
- With appropriate pricing

What I wish I had known when I was younger?
That my elders have the great wisdom of experience, whether they be manual workers, professionals, executives or colleagues (even parents!). Listen ask and learn. They know a lot more than you and will be pleased to share but only if you listen, heed, and put into practice. Otherwise you will be ignored and will have to find out for yourself but trying and failing is a great teacher! More wasteful than listening and heeding but more memorable! In the workplace the best ideas come from those closest to the task not necessarily from management or even bright young graduates!

My Personal Mantra
Do the best you can with integrity.

Comic Moment (one of many)
As a young supervisor I arrived at work early one morning to be confronted by, Dave, the janitor, a short rather smelly, illiterate 55 year old with an extremely limited expletive littered vocabulary. Brandishing a paint scraper in my face he demanded, 'What are you goin to do abart it? Every ****** mornin I 'av to do it. You're management and you got ta ******well fix it!' 'Fix what?' I politely and cautiously asked. 'Cum wi me,' I followed on with some trepidation as we headed to the male toilets.

He pushed open the door of one of the cubicles and pointed with the paint scraper into the white pan. There, proudly with its head standing out of the water and with its tail disappeared round the bend was the biggest turd I had ever seen. 'Evry mornin, wont flush away, I 'av to chop *****ing thing up wi this!' And he brandished the paint scraper in my face. You're management and you go ta ******well fix it!' He looked at me a bit old fashioned and continued, 'Wot ya goin to do abart it, Mr Manager?' Non-plussed I was thinking fast. 'You know we have some building contractors on site? Well it is almost certainly one of those and when the work is finished at the end of this week, they will leave and the problem will be solved,' I postulated. He gave a very disbelieving smile but there was a level of understanding between us and I couldn't help but add, 'You know these builders wipe their arses on cement bags and that is what causes all the trouble. We will be ok next week!' I turned on my heel and was off wondering whether management was for me or not. After the weekend the problem went away. Lucky? Probably, but my reputation was made with Dave!

Advice for young people starting out in the world
Much of this advice is contained above but in addition to integrity and listening skills, avoid personal debt. We live in an instant society, but learn patience and to wait until you can afford to purchase the things you want. Budget carefully, cover your living imperatives, shelter, food, and travel to work. Save to accumulate a minimum of six months accessible cash on which to live in the event of no income. Then and only then spend on wants. Avoid debt, it ruins lives and relationships

PHATSARA CHITTASENEE

Executive Director, Polaris Line Co.,Ltd

Polaris Line Co., Ltd is a leading freight forwarding company in Thailand. The company was established in 1990 with its main mission as freight broker, custom house brokerage and inland transportation company with me as the founder and Executive Director of Polaris Line responsible for sales, marketing as well as business operation.

Like any big corporation, all must take that first small step. Polaris started out as a freight forwarder focusing on small and medium apparel exporters who export their products from Thailand to the Middle East. Through an untiring effort to develop and expand the market, Polaris now control over 100,000 containers, exporting annually from Thailand to worldwide destinations and have become the leading freight forwarder in Thailand.

Our success is driven by three things. First is customer-focus. We keep developing our product network in line with customers' requirement. Second, we devote a lot of time and energy to building up a personal network. Not only with customers but we also develop a strong partnership with our suppliers which helps us to maintain a high quality service. In addition, the partnership mentality would not materialize without the sincerity, loyalty and constant mutual commitment. Lastly, we are performance oriented or second to none, this mentality is the third factor and we work untiringly to achieve this objective in all work we do.

Through my career-experience, I found you would sometimes be faced with difficult and complex situations where there seems to be no way out. But by surrounding yourself with a good network of colleagues, experts, coupled with your own wisdom, there will always be a solution on how to steer out of those difficulties. And after every crisis, you will come out even stronger. Thus, my personal Mantra is to be hard-working, sincere and loyal.

Despite being so focused on the quality of our work and working hard to get our job done, I never ignore that at the end of the day, it is a people business. We are tough on the problems that come in along the way of work but we always have fun as a part of our working culture. So, sharing funny stories, pictures and getting together is the key to our network building.

For young people who are just starting out in the world of business, my advice would be the following:
• Dedication and always striving to be the best.
• Surround yourself with wise and knowledgeable people; they would be a good and powerful social network supporting your business growth.
• Keep looking for better ways of doing things. Remember there is no superior thing in the business world; it can always be done better.

TONY COLLINS

Chief Executive Officer of Virgin Trains

Profession/short job description:
Chief Executive Officer of Virgin Trains

How did you make your first steps to success, and what do you consider to be the key to your success?
The key to success is to put yourself in a position which challenges you as an individual, your skills and your abilities. It is not about being better than anyone else.

What have been your most valuable career-defining experiences?
It's realising that people make businesses successful and not processes.

What advice would you have for young people just starting out in the world of business?
Remember you have been given two ears and only one mouth for a reason – Listen twice as much as you talk.

Is there anything else that you would like to add?
Success doesn't just happen, it is not a right, it comes from hard work.

GRAHAM DODRIDGE

Chief Executive, Silver Agency

Profession/short job description:
I grew up drawing pictures and remember, as a child, strangely designing advertisements for John Player Special cigarettes. I went to art school at 16 and immediately realised my vocation – 'graphic design'. Today I run a brand and advertising agency called Silver which began life in 2006. My job description extends from making the tea and vacuuming the floor to presenting the sales pitch. My mother reminds me that I once told her that I would never work for a living, but just do what I enjoy – 'Job', 'work'. These words are for other people. I just 'do'.

How did you make your first steps to success, and what do you consider to be the key to your success?
I grew up in the country and went to London to become a graphic designer. I walked the streets with my portfolio, knocking on doors with a logo on a plaque outside. I got my break in West Street, between Covent garden and Soho. A 'one man band' called John Walsh Creative took me on as his assistant. Following his lunch time pints in the Lamb and Flag, he would send me to meetings on my own. I loved putting my creative skills against a brief, eager to please and gain approval of my peers. After a year or so I began to pick up clients of my own and so struck out on my own. At 26 I started my own agency 'proper' called Gyro which 17 years later, employs 500 staff in offices all around the world.

What have been your most valuable career-defining experiences?
In 1991 at the beginning of my agency life we approached our Bank Manager, Jean Bradbury at Lloyds bank who declined a business loan request for £10K seed funding, despite an extensively crafted business plan. We promised Jean, that despite her refusal we would hold double that amount on deposit within three months. Jean agreed to buy dinner if we could manage this and three months later we ate burgers at Tootsies!

What do you wish you had known when you were younger?
To be young and unencumbered by the clutter of mid life responsibilities is the major joy of youth. I love the clutter of mid life, being the daddy of the family and the bloke who drives the car on holiday, but taking off on a motorbike to discover what's around the next corner, without a care in the world is the preserve of youth. Life is not a race. Take your time and enjoy every step.

Do you have a personal Mantra?
Take the time to watch the leaves appear in spring. I try to be a good father, husband, son, brother, boss and friend and enjoy my good fortune.

Are there any funny / comic moments that you can remember from your career?
Funny things happen everyday and I look forward to something funny happening tomorrow. I once dressed as Christopher Columbus to pitch for the marketing of the World Trade Centre in New York. Standing in a pub in Olympia in pantaloons, buckle shoes and a ostrich feather hat, next to a group of burly builders has to figure in there somewhere. We got the gig and produced marketing in the UK, France, Germany and Japan. I wanted to cry as I sat alone in my apartment in San Francisco when the great towers fell.

What advice would you have for young people just starting out in the world of business?
Make the tea. Vacuum the carpet. Tell the truth. Work hard. Enjoy the day. What will be, most certainly will be.
Is there anything else that you would like to add?
I'm off to bed now as I've got an early start in the morning. I'm going to a packaging factory and I've never been to a packaging factory before. I know I will enjoy a greasy spoon tomorrow morning, somewhere off the M1, and later I will meet some lovely new people doing something different to me. I can't wait.

www.silver-worldwide.com

JAMES DYSON

Founder & Managing Director of Dyson

Why did you decide to pursue a career in your industry?
My parents were both classicists, so there was no expectation that I would be interested in designing and making things. As a child I made the usual paper aeroplanes and tree houses and was always very interested in how things worked. But it wasn't until I was studying furniture design at the Royal College of Art that I came across design engineering and realised that this was where my real passion lay.

How did you make your first steps to success, and what do you consider to be the key to your success?
Perseverance. It took me five years, 5,127 prototypes, lots of cursing, bangs and crashes, and a rollercoaster ride from euphoria to disappointment and back again, before my vacuum cleaner was ready for market. I truly believe that to be successful, you must never give up.

What have been your most valuable career-defining experiences?
Jeremy Fry, founder of Rotork, gave me my first break. I had no experience but he must have seen some potential and gave me my first job. With Jeremy as a mentor, I learned that with enthusiasm and doggedness, anything was possible. If it didn't work one way then I was told to simply try it a different way until it did work.

Forty years on, I'm now passionate about the potential of young people. So at Dyson, we have a policy of welcoming graduates straight from the lecture theatre into the lab. We value the attitude they have and we want to put it to good use straightaway and not have them wasting time making tea for everyone (unless they're getting one themselves!) or shadowing their boss for a year before they're allowed to make anything themselves.

What do you wish you had known when you were younger?
Each mistake is a vital step towards true innovation. As Thomas Edison once said: "I have not failed, I've just found 10,000 ways that won't work." It's a hard lesson to learn but one has to accept that you don't get things working overnight. There's no such thing as a 'Eureka' moment. Getting a product right can take weeks, months, even years. Sometimes it's tempting to call it a day, to stick with what you've got, but for some of us, there's that nagging feeling that there's still a better way to do it. Even today at Dyson, the engineers take an iterative approach to design engineering; one small change at a time. A mistake or failure is just as valuable as a success – it's one step nearer to discovery.

Do you have a personal Mantra?
To be honest I don't have a personal mantra, however, I am a firm believer in wrong thinking. By that I mean people should think things out fresh and not just accept conventional ways of doing things.

What advice would you have for young people who aspire to be entrepreneurs?
Over the years, I've been referred to as an entrepreneur, which, as an engineer, I find somewhat peculiar since it's a term usually linked with the business world. However, it derives from the French verb 'entreprendre' which means 'to undertake' or, to put it simply, 'to do'. As my days are filled with 'doing' perhaps I am one after all. So for those who like 'to do' I would say:

• Be an innovator. You need to make sure that your product is different and better than anything else out there. People want value for money, even more so during a recession, and will pay a premium if they can see that they're getting a superior design that will last.
• When you've got a good idea, never give up on it. So much potential can be lost when people don't move on from their first, second or tenth knockback.
• Don't be afraid to think differently. That's how change can really happen.
• If you can do it on your own. I funded and manufactured the dual cyclone vacuum cleaner myself. It can be tough and it can get very lonely, but the rewards are greater than signing away your hard work to someone else. If you show total belief in your invention it helps others to catch on.
• Celebrate mistakes. You can always learn much more from your mistakes than your successes.

What further aspirations do you have for the Dyson Company?

It's imperative that Dyson always continues to design forward thinking technology and never looks back. In Britain there's a real appetite for retro products, which manufacturers are responding to with designs that were around 30 years ago. But to me it's a stylistic recreation of a bygone era. To ensure Dyson is constantly moving forward we invest heavily in RDD. And in spite of the fact that there is often no return of investment for a decade, I believe it is completely worthwhile, because you can be sure of a satisfied customer in the long term.

And with the James Dyson Foundation's (JDF), we want to challenge young peoples' assumptions that a career in engineering is dull and dirty. Through the JDF workshops and the James Dyson Award, we want to rekindle their fascination for technology and teach them to see beyond how something looks and investigate how it works and how it could work better.

TONY FYFE

Managing Director of Fyfes Vehicle
and Engineering Supplies Ltd

My name is Tony Fyfe and I am Managing Director of Fyfes Vehicle and Engineering Supplies Ltd, a third generation business located in Northern Ireland which leads the local market in the supply of products to garages and fabricators.

The main focus of my job is to lead and motivate the company as a whole to success through my small management team. To achieve this goal my day to day focus is development, motivation and guidance of the management team to success in their specific areas of responsibility while working with each other. The team consists of a Sales Director, a Business Development Manager, Purchasing Manager, Administration Manager, Warehouse and Logistics Manager and a Human Resources Manager. We also use a consultant, a Professor of Accountancy who meets with me at least fortnightly and I find him useful in providing an objective view as he is not as closely involved with the various   issues as myself. Although not a day to day matter I am also responsible for setting the strategy of the company, taking key decisions in consultation with relevant managers. In addition as in common with all MD's I am responsible for all matters effecting the company which are legislated on such as employment law and the various returns required on Health and Safety etc.

My first steps to success were in choosing to go University in Dublin rather than stay on in Northern Ireland. At Trinity College I met a much greater diversity of people which helped to give me a broader view on people and their capabilities. When considering a career path before graduation in the early eighties the options were fairly limited for graduates of Business Studies .The economy both North and South was depressed and many graduates emigrated to seek careers in the UK, the States or Australia. Many from my faculty who stayed on in Ireland decided to pursue careers in accountancy which involved more years of study before earnings would start to show a significant increase. My father had been pressing me to join him with the implied suggestion that if successful I could one day run the business. I had no great desire to emigrate or to spend more years studying nor had I any particular desire to go into the motor trade but I was interested in business so on balance and taking into account the fact that the company had given our family a good living to date I decided I would join Fyfes. But before doing so I took a sabbatical which I used to work in businesses in related areas to ours. In some ways I drifted into a family business but at the same time the actual decision to join was a clearly considered one and when taken I didn't join straight away but took the time out to learn from other business first. This demonstrated one key to my success namely weigh up the big decisions carefully and try to envisage their long term implications. Don't rush the big decisions.

My most valuable career-defining experiences were the sudden death of my father and the resignation of my General Manager. My fathers' death was a shock and an emotional loss which took time to recover from. At that time I was a sales rep for the company and had to quickly take on a more responsible role. About a year and a half later on return from my honeymoon, I received a letter of resignation from the companies General Manager. He had been approached by a larger company to run their Northern Ireland operation and while he may had have hopes of being appointed MD of Fyfes, he had seen over the past year or so that I was here to stay as MD.
Both of these experiences from a business perspective were a shock and taught me that you can't be prepared for shocks and therefore in business you should never be too reliant on individuals and no matter how valuable those individuals are, the Company is bigger than. Ultimately you are the key in the company and its success will largely depend on your actions and decisions. A good management team has a greater chance of long term success than one or two very talented managers.

The things I wish I had known when I was younger are too numerous to mention. From a business perspective, the one thing in particular that I believe is only learnt with maturity is the fact that I didn't know it all and while it may sound trite success really is built on teamwork. A good leader will have the wisdom to know that he can't do it all on his own. Also I wish I had recognised the importance of networking in business at an earlier age.

In all honesty, I don't have a personal mantra but if I were to have one it would simply be "Do your best and then try harder"

Unfortunately there are no funny moments that I can remember from my career that I would care to put in writing!

Advice for young people starting out in the world would be do not rush into a career path. Take time out after college to travel and try working in different businesses. You may think that you know a lot but you can be sure that as you get older you will know more; so listen to advice from older people who you trust to have your best interests at heart. In business every individual is replaceable. A team is more difficult to replace so aim to be the builder and leader of a successful team.

THOMAS GLOCER

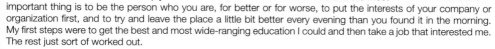

Chief Executive Officer of Reuters Corporation

How did you make your first steps to success (in particular becoming CEO of Thomson Reuters), and what do you consider to be the key to your success?
I don't believe in cookie cutter advice or the penchant of successful executives to write how-to books that others can simply follow to achieve similar success. I believe the most important thing is to be the person who you are, for better or for worse, to put the interests of your company or organization first, and to try and leave the place a little bit better every evening than you found it in the morning. My first steps were to get the best and most wide-ranging education I could and then take a job that interested me. The rest just sort of worked out.

What have been your most valuable career-defining experiences?
Probably my first operating job at Reuters which was to run our small but demanding business in Latin America. This required a lot of agility and cultural sensitivity and allowed me to make mistakes and learn from them.

What do you wish you had known when you were younger?
That people my age actually prefer individuals with character rather than some image of the perfect executive.

Do you have a personal mantra?
My personal mantra is not to have a personal mantra.

Are there any funny / comic moments that you can remember from your career?
There are many to choose from. Perhaps the most amusing in retrospect was to have been woken up at 5 in the morning to hear that our Sao Paulo office was in the process of burning down, jumping on a plane and spending the rest of the week begging for temporary office space.

What advice would you have for young people just starting out in the world of business?
Don't take a job you're not interested in and always follow the path that excites you the most, you will inspire others and be more successful.

How do you deal with the stresses of work?
Get plenty of exercise.

In your opinion, what qualities are demanded of person in your position?
Honesty, judgment and an ability to make decisions under conditions of uncertainty.

Is there anything else that you would like to add?
I think it's great that a bunch of year 12 students are interested enough in business to undertake this project and I wish you all great success.

MARTIN GRAHAM

President & CEO of Metro Retail Supply

My name is Martin Graham and I am the President & CEO of Metro Retail Supply Chain Solutions in the business of providing outsourced logistics services. What's that, I hear you saying? Well, in simple terms, it's planning, implementing and controlling the efficient flow of materials / product between the point of origin and the point of consumption in order to meet customers' demands (Supply Chain Management) – you did ask..! In my terms it's the management of the stuff moved by trucks, planes, trains, ships and stored in warehouses – that's better!

Having undertaken a four year sandwich degree in Industrial Studies at Sheffield Polytechnic (now Sheffield Hallam University) I discovered the world of transport and logistics while working at ICI during my work experience year. A real people industry with little or no graduate interest, an industry that can easily be regarded the largest in the UK with no recognition in academia and an industry almost invisible to young people looking for a career. This is changing but slowly and represents a great opportunity for you. Sandwich degrees are without doubt a real opportunity to explore possible career options whilst also building solid work experience.

During my first few years as a management trainee and junior manager I worked every job, every shift, every hour needed and was prepared to move at a moments notice. It gave me the broadest possible experience and by 25, I was managing my own distribution operation of over 150 people and at age 27 a site of over 500. It paid off. I hear many young people saying, "I don't want to work nights, I don't want to move, I don't want to do that, it doesn't interest me" - well it depends what you want to achieve.

At 30 I put everything on the line to do a Management Buy Out (MBO) – a great move and one of the best learning experiences. In January 1989 I bought the business, moved house and got married – nine months later, yes you guessed it, we sold the business…! So what did I learn?
• It's about making decisions – even if occasionally wrong ones. Make the tough calls and if this impacts on peoples jobs treat them with honesty and absolute respect.
• Cash flow is as important as profit.
• People make the difference – a great team achieve great success.

At 35, I went to Canada as Executive Vice President (grand title for a business with only $4m turnover to re-energise and build a business from ground up). A strange move to many people as it required me to move from a high profile corporate position to relative obscurity. In four years with a great team we were growing fast and the turnover had already reached $300m and went on to over $1bn. I left Canada to run the companies European operations only to join a venture capital acquisition and find myself back between the UK and Canada today.
Logistics is a great career if you want to work in a people industry, you enjoy travel and want to work / support some of the worlds' best known businesses.
So what advice do I have for young people:
• Experience can't be bought or taught - grab all opportunities and start early. Saturday jobs and holiday work of the most basic sort are experiences that can never be repeated. Management books are a great opportunity for reflection and only that.
• Its always about people as customers, colleagues or friends (the most junior person in your organisation is important and deserves respect)
• Remember there is no such thing as can't.
• Life is to be lived – make sure you enjoy your work. Sometimes this is your responsibility.
• Challenges are opportunities – the chance for you and or your team to excel.

My mantra – any problem can be solved. Sometimes this is achieved by doing nothing but nearly always needs the input and support of those around you.

NEIL GRANT

National Account Manager, Comma Oil and Chemical Ltd

My name is Neill Grant, I am employed by Comma Oil and Chemicals Ltd, a subsidiary of the global energy giant, Exxon Mobil. My role within the organisation is a National Account Manager, which primarily entails organising product promotions, setting up trading relationships, price negotiations, marketing, product range reviews, introducing new products to market and also dealing with the day to day issues and needs of a National purchasing group. Needless to say, there's never a dull day!

I suppose I began my route to success many years ago with an HND in business management at a local college in Scotland, which looking back was the single most important thing I have done, further education. Nothing beats it for getting onto the first rung of the ladder to success. For me it wasn't necessarily the subject I did, I have had a few jobs since leaving college some of which had little relevance to the course. As an example, I was a Police Officer for Northamptonshire Police for 4 years, what that's got to do with running your own business I have no idea, even now. Keeping up to date with your paperwork might have some relevance. That's not a whinge by the way. Self-discipline is something further education brings to your make up, and will help you throughout your working life.

I was involved with sports clubs and societies whilst at college, and made many friends, many of whom I still keep in touch with today, they all went off to do different things. Family businesses, builders, teachers, electricians, most have helped me somewhere along the way. Never forget your friends is what I'm saying here. You can do any job you like after college/university, its up to you. You're qualified! Companies love to see qualifications against your name, it's the biggest door opener going. Never miss the chance of further education, no matter what anyone tells you, life will be a lot more rewarding when you're earning a good salary. The whole world can open up for you then. Ever heard the song "money makes the world go round"? It does. I only really started understanding what life was all about when i got out of my cocoon at college and into the big bad world of business. I never worried about what other people thought of me, I just looked ahead and believed in myself. Never hang around with doubters or losers, they will only drag you down.

You also need an inner belief that you are the most employable person on the planet, all you have to do then, is prove it. B*lsh*tters soon get found out, don't be one, otherwise you will have more jobs than a person who has had a lot of jobs! Sir Alan Sugar will tell you the same, watch the apprentice.

Confidence is a great asset, use it in positive way. This will come with experience and the successes you achieve during your life. However beware, overconfidence can alienate you to both your peers and seniors.

Always do what you say you're going to do, it's the only way to gain the trust and respect of the people you deal with in this world. Be sincere in all aspects of business.
I have always put 100% into everything I do whether its work, sport or family, it's the only way to think. I always think of the positives never the negatives, it's what drives me.

I am thankful for the guidance and support of my parents. We didn't always see eye to eye on things and I was a pretty headstrong individual back then, but they always wanted the best for me even if I didn't see it at the time. They have been proved right over time. Use parents to help get you where you want to be, push them as much as they push you. Challenge then in a positive way, you will be amazed how much they respond, I can only talk from experience here.

If I had one piece of advice for any young person who has a natural ability for sport, pursue your dream on the sporting field.

I had the ability to play most sports well with a particular flair for football and had trials for the Scottish Schools and Dundee FC but I chose the wrong option, I wanted money first and foremost at the time and didn't see money in football, so I worked all the hours i could in a supermarket so I had money to go out with my friends, how blind was I then, if only I knew what I know now. I could be on Beckham's money now!

Have respect for money, save more than you earn, that's the Scotsman in me talking. Use bucket loads of common sense in any given situation and you cannot fail. Having the ability to laugh at yourself has also helped me to succeed, lots of people I come into contact with take life too seriously. Keeping a level head when everyone else is losing theirs will make you stand out and be someone to be respected.

Good Luck

GUY HANDS

CEO of Terra Firma

I'm the CEO of Terra Firma, which is a large European private equity firm. Basically, we buy companies that are misunderstood or neglected by their current owners, work closely with their management to transform them into healthy businesses, and sell them for a profit after a period of roughly four to five years.

I've always been very entrepreneurial, going to back when I started a photography business when I was 14. I didn't enjoy school a great deal, but was always very interested in business, and at University, I ran a very successful art business while studying. I then bought an art gallery when I was 21, but didn't do enough research into the building because when it began to collapse the following year, I was left with a very big repair bill! The lesson I learnt here, which has been very important throughout my career, is always to know exactly what you are getting into when you make an investment.

It is an often-heard truth, but most lessons that we learn are learnt when times are hardest. I've faced a number of difficult situations in my career, but one of the trickiest has also been one of the most recent - running EMI, the record label that we bought in 2007. Working in the music industry was a very different experience from working in finance - business is much more personal there, and people said some very harsh things about the work we were doing to try to repair EMI. The lesson I've learnt from that is you need to have a strong belief that what you are doing is right, and a hard enough shell to take the knocks, but you also need to be flexible enough and open enough to hear people's criticisms and differing views.

My advice to anyone starting out in business today would be don't expect to get it right the first time, or indeed even the second time, but concentrate on doing the best you can and learning along the way. Eventually if you are good at business you will get a great opportunity.

PETER HENRY

Valeo Service UK

I left school with 4 A levels and went directly into a 2 year Commercial Training programme in the aviation industry. After moving to the automotive sector and working in export sales administration for 4 years I assumed a full sales role for a number of overseas territories, (Middle East, Africa, USA, and Canada). I spent most of my 20's travelling the world before moving into a UK Sales management position. After 3 years running a sales force I became a Sales & Marketing Director of a medium sized business aged 32 and then moved into general management 3 years later. I have spent the last 15 years as a Managing Director and currently run a business with turnover circa £35m.

This may seem like a well planned career; however in truth I was lucky and was in the right place at the right time. I didn't plan my future during my early working years and was too busy chasing women and drinking. This is an essential part of growing up and should be continued at every opportunity; however it does eventually need to be balanced with a little forethought. A change of industry gave me the chance to move into sales and start travelling the world which exposed me to numerous growth experiences. This was the point, aged 25, that I started to think ahead and set targets. I set a goal to be a Sales & Marketing Director of a medium sized company by the time I was 35 and worked and trained to be in this position.

The following are my top 10 tips :

- Don't fall or drift into a job or career. Think carefully about what you love doing and what you are good at, (usually the same thing), and look for industries or sectors that offer such roles.
- This is the best way to balance professional and personal satisfaction. Thousands of people go to work either being ambivalent about their job or actually hating what they do. Life is too short – think and plan ahead. Working and having fun is a rare commodity, but it can be done.
- However, whilst an idealistic job may seem worthy when you are young, always remember the money – life is a lot, lot easier when you have it.
- Look for opportunities to work for your-self. If you are a local plumber, builder or electrician it may not always seem as glamorous as a corporate life, but the potential to decide your own destiny and create wealth is far greater.
- Act as a sponge in your early roles – throw yourself into as many projects as possible – don't worry if you make mistakes, (as long as you don't repeat them), volunteer for everything in the company and get yourself known.
- You make your own luck by being in the right place at the right time – remember the 3 E's = education, experience and exposure.
- Always, always look the part – especially when you are the younger member of the group – it will set you apart. Also, always have a firm handshake and look the other person in the eye.
- Never compromise your personal integrity – never cheat or lie in business....you will be found out.
- If you can, always travel the world on somebody else's ticket – it is a fantastic way to open your mind to different people / cultures, aid your personal growth, live out your fantasies, (meet women), and get a tan during the winter.
- Employers look for a JEDI – judgement, empathy, drive, initiative. There is nothing more attractive to an employer than intelligence & enthusiasm, it far outweighs any risk of your youth and will move your career more quickly.

CHARLES HORTON

Profession/short job description:
I am managing director of Southeastern trains. This means that I lead and manage one of the largest train companies in the UK, providing rail services to 145 million passengers every year. Southeastern runs 1700 services every day, 182 stations, has 400 trains and 3800 employees

How did you make your first steps to success, and what do you consider to be the key to your success?
Early in my career, I was lucky enough to work with people who took an interest in my development. I was also self confident enough to stand up for what I thought was right and worked hard to learn! I had briefly been in the army after leaving school and this helped me become more self reliant and trusting of my own instincts. I did a degree and then secured a job as a graduate trainee with the London Underground. I enjoyed the experience so much that I ended up staying with them for 14 years in many different roles.

What has been most valuable career – defining experiences?
I've learned something from every job I've done. Early in my career I took every development opportunity I could and was never afraid to take sideways move so I could learn more about the business. In terms of defining moments, helping to prepare evidence for the King Cross Fire Inquiry (in which 31 people tragically died) was very harrowing but shaped my determination to ensure the railways become as safe as they can be. Also leading my first team of 100 people at 24 years of age was daunting but I got a tremendous buzz from the experience and really started to understand that the job of a manager is to get the best from your people, not necessarily to be the best player in the team!

What do you wish you had known when you were younger?
I wish I'd known that business is more than anything about building and maintaining relationships. If people trust, like and respect you, it will carry you a long way. I also wish I'd appreciated how important it is to work hard at school and get the best qualifications you can. On their own they won't get you a job, but they do help get you 'through the door' and give you the opportunity to sell yourself to employers.

What advice would you have for young people just starting out in the world of business?
Never be afraid to ask and seek out people who are good at what they do so that you can learn from them. Don't be led by the crowd and live by your own values. Never, ever think that any job is "beneath you", make the best of every role and learn everything you can from it.

Do whatever job you are given to the best of your ability. I've always had a mindset which can be best summed up as 'do it well, or don't do it at all!' My first job was cleaning a pub, I worked as hard at that as I do in my current role.

SIMON HURLEY-SMITH

Managing Director, Health Matters (UK) Limited

I own and operate a company called Health Matters employing 10 people and handle the employee health benefits of around 380 companies throughout the UK. I started the business in 1999 and I have grown it each year. We now have a combined premium income in the region of £7m and commission/fee income of around £680k.

Other than wanting the usual 'health and happiness' my one goal in life, ever since I can remember, was to be my own boss, be answerable to no one and to be financially secure.

My parents ran a shop retailing sports equipment for 25 years and I learned from an early age the importance of sales skills. My father was a great sales person and by watching and listening to him I learned how to buy and sell. Our family joke was that an unsuspecting customer came in the shop one day for a squash racket but didn't find one he liked so my dad persuaded him to ditch squash, take up badminton and sold him everything he needed to play his new sport.

I never really enjoyed school and never entertained the idea of university. All I wanted to do, was to get into the big wide world and to start making a living. So I left school at 16 and immediately became a market trader (fruit and veg not stocks and shares). At the age of 18 I was selling frogs on rocks on the sea-front in Rhyl. I'd go to the beach, pick up large pebbles and super-glue tiny green plastic frogs to them and flog them to the tourists, 3 for a quid!

Between the ages of 17 and 22 all at the same time I had a full time 'commission only' sales job, operated a small mail-order business and ran a market stall. However I was always aware that I needed a 'real' business to survive.

So after working for an Insurance company for 6 years and learning a trade I set up Health Matters and have focused my attention on building the business so that I can earn a good living and perhaps one day sell out.

I don't have any pearls of wisdom or a personal mantra that I've developed over the last 22 years, since I was 18, but I have learned that it's not particularly difficult to be in business provided you're reliable, likeable and don't act like an idiot.

There are a few facts that I have learnt along the way and these would certainly have been useful to have known when I was younger:

- People make strange decisions so don't even think about predicting what they are going to do.

- No one will do something as good as you can do it so either do it yourself or have low expectations.

- Treat everyone equally whether they are an employee, a customer or a prospect.

- Encourage your competitors to underestimate you and keep a low profile.

Sorry I can't give you anymore of an insight !

PROFESSOR MICHAEL JEFFERSON

Professor of International Business and Sustainability, Centre for International Business and Sustainability, London Metropolitan Business School, London Metropolitan University

When I was 18 I was at a West Country boarding school, where I had arrived unusually late (at almost 15). This was due to my parents having moved to the Middle East, my Father having a job out there, and occasioning my leaving a very large so-called 'public school' south of London. Six years earlier I had been summoned, like the rest of us, to a meeting of our Senior Classics Master and his No. 2. Mine was the second name read out: the second most stupid Latin pupil, so I must give up the subject and try something else. Six years on my next Headmaster was telling me that I must try for Oxbridge, and there was I telling him I didn't have the basic entry requirement of Latin. We worked on this together. I asked him: "Where will the brightest boys be trying to go for a scholarship?" "Cambridge", he replied. "So I'll try Oxford", I replied. He mentioned the various colleges which were having scholarship examinations in December, 1958. I asked him: "Which college do you think the brightest boys will be trying for?" He mentioned the first one, then the second likely choice. "Right", I said, "I'll try this second one." I had never heard of it. I went up to this college (Univ.), took the exams (and was lucky), confessed (as was obvious by my performance) that I knew no Latin, and passed the modern equivalent of GCSE in it a little later. Three wonderful years followed (though I should have worked harder), and then I went to the London School of Economics to do a postgraduate course in business administration.a postgraduate course in business administration.

There followed a decade where I mostly practised economics – in the City, as a consultant and then working with senior businessmen. This lead eventually to my being appointed Chief Economist of The Royal Dutch/Shell Group, and then some very interesting jobs in planning (including developing scenarios of possible futures), oil supply strategy, and hands-on oil supply and trading. I got a great "buzz" out of being at the leading edge of scenario development in the world; advising people, in an industry which had only known good post-war times, what the risks and opportunities of the oil "crises" of the 1970s might be; supplying up to 45% of a country's oil requirements; trying to buy tanker cargoes of crude oil more cheaply than the competition; sorting out derelict bitumen business.

By 1990 there were only a couple of jobs I was really interested in, none of which were then vacant, and I did not want to do an "external relations" job which I was offered – feeling I would have to sing from the corporate hymn book.

So I became Deputy Secretary General of the World Energy Council, which paid poorly but was challenging as it seemed stuck in the early 20th Century when I joined. For a decade I laboured to achieve change, and succeeded to some extent. For about half that time I was threatened with the sack or being silenced for, among other things, getting involved with the Intergovernmental Panel on Climate Change (many of our members were powerful fossil fuel producers/processors) and the UN Development Programme (many private sector firms were not too keen on UN agencies).

Following my departure from the World Energy Council I worked as an energy and environmental consultant – sometimes with enjoyment and sometimes with frustration (the latter epitomised by a short spell as lead consultant of the G8 Renewable Energy Task Force). I have still not worked out whether the poor communications at the top were a deliberate effort to sabotage renewable energy interests or not. I left long before a very poor final report was produced – which never even got placed before G8 Ministers' meeting in Genoa!

Over the years jobs seem to have come to me. The last serious job interview I had was in 1966, when I joined an economic consultancy with the aim of managing five economics professors and a bibulous PR man. That was fun for two years, but I would advise against working with people who drink on the job. Otherwise things just seem to have happened. My next five jobs came about by people approaching me. The latest approach came late in 2007, when I was 67 years old, to be a Professor – with a contract which takes me into my 70s. The area I cover is International Business and Sustainability. What even I find odd is that, despite being in business or on the fringes of business over a period of some 45 years, I have written quite a number of books and peer-reviewed journal papers. I like this rather unusual range of activities. I have greatly enjoyed working with some very interesting people, including those involved with the Intergovernmental Panel on Climate Change, who kindly sent me a certificate thanking me for contributing to their award of the 2007 Nobel Peace Prize. But, as all those who know me will attest, I cannot 'kow-tow' to anyone or anything if I am not convinced it is right – by which I mostly mean intellectually honest.

Looking back over the years, while I recognise I cannot change my basic mind set, I have from time to time wondered what my working life would have been if I had compromised more; been more 'clubbable'; been endowed with greater inter-personal skills. Would I have been more successful, especially in material terms? Probably. Would I now feel as much self-worth? Probably not. In the end, perhaps, the key thing which matters is to be true to oneself – for better or for worse. I think I felt that intuitively at the age of 18. I am more comfortable with that idea now, warts and all.

My work has taken me to over 60 countries. Travelling in aeroplanes, even before the days of widespread concern about greenhouse gas emissions and 9/11, is a much over-rated activity. But the opportunity to travel around the world is an important learning process. Above all, however, I thank the people who have given me the great opportunities of my life and work. That Headmaster at Kingswood School, Bath, 50 years ago and those that have followed him. Those who have believed in me. I think they have done so not because I was always easy to work with, but because I said what I genuinely believed. Also, despite that academic streak, I'm probably regarded as hard working and fairly efficient – which I was probably not aged 18!

HENRIK JENSEN

Vice President for Global Customer Service, Maersk Line

My career track takes me through a vast variety of functions, countries, and cultures.
I started my working career as Sergeant and Lieutenant in the Danish Army and gained my first leadership training there.
I subsequently started my career with A.P.Moller Maersk and throughout my 18 years have had the following positions/postings:

- Management trainee in Copenhagen, Denmark – various functional training
- Arabic Studies, Cairo, Egypt (4 months)
- Marketing Assistant, Kuwait (Sales, Customer service)
- Line Manager, Johannesburg, South Africa (Sales, Operations, Customer Service)
- Owner's Representative, Alexandria, Egypt (Office Manager)
- Managing Director, Riga, Baltic States
- Line Manager, Bangkok, Thailand (Sales, Operations, Customer Service)
- Area Line Manager, Singapore, South East Asia (Pricing, Operations, Marketing)
- Managing Director, Malaysia & Singapore
- Vice President, Global Customer Service, Copenhagen

Success is an individual measure and what some define as success, others don't. It is consequently difficult to claim being successful to a broader audience. My view is that as long as you follow your own personal conviction and are true to yourself you can be successful. Whether the result is success in terms of career progression, money, family life, or other aspects is not important as long as you have integrity towards yourself.

My professional career has been driven by a desire to learn about different cultures, live in different countries, and to lead others. I believe that having an open inquisitive mind to life in general and to other nationalities, religions is if not a prerequisite then at the very least a big advantage to being successful in an international business environment. My biggest learning came from being sent abroad to Egypt at the age of 20 to study Arabic in preparation to a posting in Kuwait. By exploring the country, the people, the traditions, etc I learned that by having a positive mindset and entering dialogue from a positive angle you can achieve and learn more that you ever expected.

A good career and a successful career path does not come without a lot of hard work. There are no free lunches. However, if you are willing to put in some extra effort and learn to delegate and follow up the working hours do not necessarily have to be crazy.
The most important aspects of being a successful leader, apart obviously from functional, management, and leadership skills are strong values. These can be different from person to person and from company to company, but what I believe in are:

- Personal integrity. You need to keep your promises otherwise no-one will trust you and no-one will follow you.
- Treat people with respect
- Humility

My advise to young people starting out in a corporate career or with an own company is:

- Have an open mind to other people, also when they are different from yourself.
- Get experience from living abroad.
- Be true to yourself and your surroundings. Don't lose your personal integrity.

Chris Johnson

Chief Executive of Paragon Electronic Ltd

Profession, short job description

I am the Chief Executive of Paragon Electronics Ltd. This is the holding company for the Paragon Electronics Group. The business was started by myself and my business partner in 1991 and today employs around 350 people across 3 sites, two in the UK and one in the Czech Republic. We supply logistics and manufacturing services to industrial, military and medical businesses.

How did you make your first steps to success?

My first business venture was shortly after leaving school when I went in to partnership with a friend building competition slalom canoes.

What Have been your most valuable career defining experiences?

That first business was a valuable lesson... in everything you shouldn't do in business: going in to a partnership with someone you don't know that well, no business plan, no money, just a rough idea. After 18 months of having fun and financing my canoeing activities on the back of the business I left to get a proper job! Bizarrely this turned out to be in the electronics industry (my Physics teacher at school would not have believed this possible!) I have remained in that industry all my working life.

What do you wish you had known when you were younger?

All the things I know now! The experiences of working with different people form all works of life, from the shop floor to senior managers, from different industries, different countries and different cultures is invaluable, you never stop learning. All of these experiences help to provide an increasingly sound basis for future decision making and help you to understand more about yourself and other people. In business people are always your greatest asset and the key to any successful venture.

Do you have a personal mantra?

I remember reading a book called The Water Babies (by Charles Kingsley) when I was really very young and being struck by one of the characters in that book. I remember her as a fearsome creature "mrs Do As You Would Be Done By"..... I have always tried to practice that in my business career.....be firm but fair.

Are there any funny moments from your career?

Thousands but I'm not sure any of them would get printed! In business, as in life, it is important to have fun but never take yourself too seriously!

What advice would you have for young people starting out in the world?

Get the best education you can, but don't panic if you don't know what you want to do when you leave school or university. Get yourself as much experience as you can, apply yourself diligently to everything you do and develop from there.

In my experience hard work is always rewarded........eventually! So be patient, be honest with yourself and if you make mistakes (and you will) learn the lessons each and every time.

SARAH LU

Youdoo

Sarah Lu graduated from Buckinghamshire University in 2001 with a degree in Graphic Design & Illustration, aged 20. In 2001, she moved to Brighton and worked in various bars, and did horrible cleaning jobs whilst setting up her own design agency called 'Shortlong Graphics' (named after the infamous 80s mullet hair-do) with the financial help and support of the Prince's Trust.

Shortlong had clients such as CND, The Keep Britain Tidy Group and Brighton Natural Health Centre but in 2002 it ceased trading due to a lack of understanding in business. Its clients however, were still looked after by Sarah Lu who worked with them as a freelance designer instead, whilst managing her own pub franchise.

In 2005 and after working day and night to save up £15K for the start up of her new business (later to be known as Youdoodoll) she decided that there was one more thing she had to do first...

And that was to jet set to New York and work for top advertising agencies such as Cunning and Naked Communications. Here she learnt about life, the 'rat-race', Manhattan and most importantly, marketing and advertising.

In 2007, Sarah Lu set up Youdoodoll Ltd (from the idea through to the branding, marketing and even the packaging) and after a selling 840 Youdoodolls at a trade show (which made £8K in a week), she knew it was time to enter BBC2's Dragons' Den, a programme where entrepreneurs are face to face with some of the biggest investors in the UK...

Sarah Lu's inspirations come from a love of the 80s. Retro toys and other distinguishable memorabilia, such as the 'Rubix Cube' and 'Guess Who?'. There's also the music, the fashion, but most importantly, the low-tech, simple yet clever and outrageously creative ways of that time. We all loved Blue Peter, didn't we?

How did you make your first steps to success, and what do you consider to be the key to your success?

When I was 11 I told myself that I'd be a millionaire by the time I was 25... Hmm, seems a very long time ago now and maybe I was a little naïve. Of course at that age I was selling hand made cards and t-shirts that I'd hand crafted with fabric paints, so a few pounds felt like a thousand pounds.

I remember dad leaving for work in the evenings straight after dinner. He worked night shifts at a factory. I remember his unhappy face, clock watching and counting down the seconds before having to leave his family. I vowed never to clock watch. I also vowed never to be in a situation where hours and hours of work paid for just a few hours of living my life.

My parents were refugees, boat people from Vietnam who sought refuge over here in England. Life was difficult and later on Dad left, so it was even harder.

I think I was determined at a young age to have a job doing something I enjoyed, and that made me enough money to survive so that I could look after my mum and my younger siblings.
The only way I could think of achieving this was by being self-employed.

What have been your most valuable career-defining experiences?

It is uncanny how the things that seem to go wrong at the time (the situations that really make you frustrated and feel like you're stuck in a hole) are the ones that build you, teach you the best lessons and funnily enough, open up the best doors.

When Shortlong was in its last stages, I was heartbroken and vowed never to work in design again. My boyfriend at the time, who had a good hot-shot job in TV, dumped me because his life was moving and mine was stagnant. A horrible state of affairs, but I ended up losing everything that was dear to me and it turned out to be the best thing ever. I picked myself up, re-jigged the company so that I was a free-lancer, worked as a pub manager (something that was flexible, well paid and also something that I didn't care about enough to engulf me) and I started planning my future product design company and saved up money to invest in my ideas.

I entered a competition with National Endowment for Science, Technology and the Arts (NESTA), their pioneer competition. I really thought this was it and my life would be turned around - I drew up all my ideas, wrote my business plans, and I passed each leg of the competition. I was on a roll! Then in the last leg, I lost. So I ran away to New York and ended up working for some of the best advertisement agencies at that time. I learnt so much.

Then I came back and I thought to myself, I may have not won a place at NESTA but I'm half way to my dream of having a product design company, so I thought "What the hell, I'll do it myself."

I managed to get Youdoodoll up and running, sales under my belt and clients such as Topshop and Iwantoneofthose.com and I wanted to expand but without any finances, I decided to cut my losses and I entered the BBC television programme 'Dragons Den'.

Youdoodoll Limited was founded in June 2007. This past year and a half have been the most difficult, exciting and rewarding so far, and I am eager to do more. This is my first real business and I know it won't be my last. I'm already planning the next two.

I like to challenge myself by setting high goals. That's what I am good at - problem solving and achieving my aims.

What do you wish you had known when you were younger?
Things take time.

I wish that had I known that each time things did not go as planned, or when I was forced to go off track, that the lessons I had learnt would have made me into who I am today.

I wish I had known that my experiences were valuable 'career-defining' experiences.

Do you have a personal Mantra?
"If you build it, they will come," (said in a deep manly voice)

Yes, I've ripped off Kevin Costner's 'Field of Dreams'… Ha ha! I can't think of one for myself, I've never been asked if I have one. Hmm… I will now have to think of one for myself!

Are there any funny / comic moments that you can remember from your career?
Creative advertising is a funny world to get into and a very sought after. Its bad enough if you do not have the training, or the contacts, or a portfolio of advertising, so trying to get a 'creative's' job in New York was no mean feat!

I knew that I wouldn't get very far and I had heard that creatives do not take to designers much, so I was in for a treat.

I decided that to get my foot in the door, I needed to think laterally, not literally. That's what I was once told at university.

I made home-less style posters of myself and pinned them all over Manhattan (outside the offices of the creative studios on my hit list) and I also made life sized cardboard cut outs of myself and placed them in Creative Director's offices all around New York with the words "Try before you buy! Look how great I'd look in your office" scrawled across them.

I was stopped at customs on the way into New York – They were quite amused at my hand luggage!

I was also chased down the street by NYPD for 'fly-postering' illegally – I had no idea!

What advice would you have for young people just starting out in the world?
Always give yourself the chance to say that you have tried. Trying means at least giving it a go 3 times!

Is there anything else that you would like to add?
Remember that being successful is up to you.

PETER MARKS

Chief Executive of the Co-operative Group

Peter Marks is the Chief Executive of The Co-operative Group, one of the world's biggest consumer co-operatives. The Group employs more than 70,000 staff and has more than 4,000 stores and branches across the UK including convenience food stores, pharmacies, travel branches and funeral homes.

When I was young I never had any thought about what I wanted to be or where I wanted to go in life.

My parents were working-class. My father was a semi-skilled engineer who worked overtime to make ends meet but never really felt he had succeeded, however hard he tried. My mother had four of us to raise, two boys and two girls (I was the eldest boy). Financially, we were always stretched.

My parents were ambitious for me, especially my father. They hoped that I would become a teacher, doctor or lawyer, something professional. The most important thing for them was that I did better than they had done in life.

I passed my eleven-plus and that secured me a place at the local Catholic Grammar School in Bradford. But it was my parents who had the ambitions for me, not myself. It was the 1960s and as a teenager I was more interested in The Beatles and The Rolling Stones than I was in academic work or making a career for myself.

I flunked most of my 'O' levels getting just four when my teachers knew I should have done much better. I just hadn't worked hard enough. I started in the sixth form retaking my exams and starting 'A' levels but my heart wasn't in it. I just wasn't motivated by academic work. I wanted to earn some money like many of my friends who'd left school already. Going to university was the last thing on my mind. In fact at that stage I could have easily gone off the rails.

It was around that time, I started working on a Saturday at a local grocer's store near our home. Soon after it was bought by the Bradford and District Co-operative Society and the new manager took a shine to me and suggested I take a full-time job. I hated school with a vengeance by then and told my mum and dad I wanted to work at the Co-op instead! My parents went spare. They seemed to think that I'd let them down and that I was a failure. I'll never forget the rows we had.

But one day my dad came home with a copy of the Daily Mirror and there was an article about how a supermarket manager could earn as much as a bank manager. So perhaps retailing could offer me a professional career after all. It was enough to make my dad relent.

However, my parents hadn't given up on me continuing my education. When I started work at the Co-op full-time, I also started studying at college in Huddersfield two nights a week for the Institute of Grocery Distribution qualification (which covered everything from learning the different cuts of meat to the latest techniques of food store management). I then went on to study for my Ordinary and Higher National Certificates in business studies. I remember my first area manager was a gentleman named Albert Drake. Albert was ex-army and very strict. It was from him that I learnt the importance of having high personal standards of appearance and being disciplined in my work.

I relished the opportunity I'd been given to be the boss. I enjoyed seeing tangible results being achieved, of having sales and profit figures to study. I realised I had missed this side of business life although I had learnt a great deal from working in Personnel. I went on to run our department stores, Travel business and Food stores, before eventually becoming Chief Executive of Yorkshire Co-operative Society. Following mergers between different co-ops, in 2007, I became Chief Executive of The Co-operative Group.

It's not until you sit behind the desk that you appreciate the enormity of the responsibility you have as a Chief Executive. The future of the business is in your hands. The employees are relying on me for their jobs. The Board of Directors is relying on me to deliver our objectives. Members are relying on me to act in their interests. In the first few days you are struck by the enormity of it. And it can be lonely...because it's down to you. But then you realise that you have to work through your team and you have to develop a team ethic. Picking the best people to help run the business is vital and delegation is also important.

In my view, you need to understand what it's like to work at the bottom of the business you are running. Too many bosses haven't experienced that. I couldn't do my job as well as our results suggest I am, if I hadn't worked my way up from the bottom.

The fear of failure I mentioned earlier plays out in how I work each day. I can still wake up at 3am thinking about a big decision I have to make. But you grow in confidence. You learn to relax and to believe in your own ability and the ability of those around you. But I never escape that fear and that need to succeed.

For me success has always been about commercial success – sales, profit, driving down our costs. But working within the Co-operative Movement has given me other priorities as well. I've learnt that a business must offer values, as well as value to its customers.

If anything positive can be said to have come out of the current global financial crisis, it must be the profound reminder that ethics in business do matter. At The Co-operative Group, business ethics are woven into our DNA. Our whole model of operating is about serving the needs of our members and giving them a democratic say in how the business is run, as a well as giving them a share in the profits. That's important to me and it's why I have stayed in the Co-operative Movement.

Looking back I can see that being the eldest son had an effect on me. The expectations on me from my father were greater than for my siblings. And I can see that I inherited from my father a fear of failure. That fear has driven me over the years to succeed.

So I progressed through each of the departments in the store. Butchery I remember well, as I used to cut myself frequently and was a regular visitor to the Bradford Royal Infirmary to have stitches on my hands! I soon felt I was ready to run a big store of my own by then and was rather disappointed that my first manager's job was for a small store in a run down area of Bradford. I was 21 years old and thought I knew it all. But of course I didn't.
I made plenty of mistakes in that first job. I suffered from the arrogance of youth! You had to be vigilant. You had to have an eye for detail. You couldn't give blind trust or be too casual about how you delegated work. But you have to make mistakes to learn and you also have to give other people the opportunity to succeed.

Eventually I progressed to larger stores and for some years worked in Personnel, eventually heading the department and joining the Society's senior management team. I had a habit of speaking my mind about how the business was doing and on one occasion was particularly critical of how we were running our Funeral homes. The Deputy Chief Executive gave me the chance to put my money where my mouth was and I found myself running the Funerals business.

I'd like to be remembered for taking the Co-operative back to the top flight of retailing. For most of my career we've been declining commercially and losing the respect of our customers and competitors. I want to be remembered for taking us back to the premiership, back to strength. So we are loved by our customers and admired by our competitors.

If I had the chance to speak to myself as a young man I would say: "Be determined and overcome obstacles, don't be afraid to make mistakes but make sure you learn from them."

My dad used to say: "Never look down on people on the way up, as you might meet them again on the way down." In other words give people respect for who and what they are. If you do that, and you work hard at something you love, then I believe you will also gain the respect you deserve.

ADRIAN MCGLYNN

Company Secretary & Director of Weatherbys

Profession/short job description:

Company Secretary and Director of Weatherbys – a group of companies providing administrative, banking and other commercial services to the British horseracing and breeding industry.

How did you make your first steps to success, and what do you consider to be the key to your success?

I suspected from an early age that academic success would give me more freedom to choose what I wanted to pursue as a career.

So I engaged in collecting O and A levels both in number and high grade. I had absolutely no idea at 18 what path I would follow, so I went to Durham University to read English Literature. Completed the degree, but aged 21, still had no real idea of what I would then do. The careers office had a very basic computer program into which you fed all sorts of information about what you were good at, bad at, and wanted from a career. It would then output various jobs for consideration. I was told that I was the first undergraduate to be told by the computer…"there are no suitable jobs for you"….I carried that report around proudly – and enrolled to do a Master's degree in English!

During that year, my 4th at Durham, I realised that the world of horseracing had taken powerful hold upon me, and that the best career for me would be one associated with horseracing. Of course, the careers office had no experience of such nonsense, so I had to make my own way.

That was the best thing and probably the defining point of my career. Whilst all my undergraduate colleagues were being sucked into positions with big companies coming to the University on the dreaded "milk round", I elected to make my own way.

There was no internet or email in those days, so it wasn't simply a matter of whizzing my CV around. I had to plan, research and call people. The governing body of the sport at that time (1989), the Jockey Club, had been making noises about wanting to recruit "bright young graduates", so I made it my task to say "here I am!"

Relentlessly, I did so. I met with dozens of people, most of whom did not have a job to offer me, but were all interested and gave me new contacts to try. It was a considerable investment of time and money, and sometimes I wondered if it wouldn't just be easier to join my University colleagues and accept the "milk round" bait and trot off on a graduate programme. But I persisted and by September, just 10 arduous weeks after leaving University, I had secured a post at the British Racing School in Newmarket. A junior, and in many ways ridiculous post for someone with a Master's in English Literature, I was paid about one third of what my fellow graduates were getting in their first positions with outfits such as Arthur Anderson, Deloitte and even Marks & Spencer.

But the good thing was that I had got a foot in the door. Horseracing was paying me! From that first moment, I knew I had done the right thing, and nothing has happened in the subsequent 20 years to dim that belief. I have carved a career path and risen to a position of seniority within a prestigious company. My work has always been interesting because it has revolved around the sport that I adore. I couldn't be a director of a company that runs golf or football, any more than be a director of a pharmaceutical company! I am definitely operating in my favoured niche.

Do you have a personal Mantra?

I have no particular mantra, but my philosophy has been a strong belief in doing something that interests, inspires and amuses. My tutor at Durham said his mantra was to find somewhere he liked to be and then see if he could persuade someone to pay him for being there. He liked being at Durham University and so became a don! So I guess that my mantra would be along the lines of finding something that I liked doing and then persuading someone to pay me for that.

It seems such a shame that as we progress through our academic careers that we focus increasingly upon the subjects we like, discarding those that we dread, but then often go into work that we do not much like. I knew that must not happen to me. It would be like taking up maths again after 4 glorious years of English Literature study!

What do you wish you had known when you were younger?
I rarely look back or regret that there were things I wish I had known earlier. I was fortunate to have guessed that academic success would propel me into a position to make career choices easier. I was also fortunate to attend a school which valued and nurtured individuality.

But I would always stress to young people the immense value of an ability to write correctly and attractively. It stands out and gets yourself noticed. I would also add the power of being articulate. Not necessarily an orator, but any ability to communicate with clarity and enthusiasm and to deny business jargon a home is most inspiring.

What advice would you have for young people just starting out in the world?
Be ambitious. Not necessarily in striving to be at the top of a business. But more in seeking satisfaction from work. There are so many opportunities now in all sorts of fascinating areas; my own world of horseracing for instance. When I traipsed around looking for a first job, racecourse management looked to be a possible route. But in 1989, most courses had a single manager, usually filled by an ex-army officer, who would stay until old age/death took hold. Now there are hundreds of people involved in managing Britain's 60 racecourses, with plenty of opportunities for young people. "Work" has never been more interesting. But often you have to put quite a bit of effort into finding the really interesting nuggets. It's then all the more satisfying.

If you find yourself dreading going to work – as I once dreaded going to maths lessons….make a change. A life of maths lessons? Unbearable!

ALEC MORGAN

Country Manager for Banner Batterien

I am the Country Manager in the UK for the Austrian Battery Manufacturer, Banner Batterien who produce original equipment quality Automotive and CV batteries for vehicle assemblers etc. and for all makes for the aftermarket.

Banner GB sells mostly to the aftermarket and mostly to wholesale independent parts distributors known as Motor Factors or even as something else by certain suppliers.

Having spent more than forty years selling into the UK aftermarket, with some years in export sales, I can say that there have been hard times before when the currency fell to around what it is today, or lower, interest rates were sky high and doom and gloom pervaded the country. However, by adapting to ever changing scenario and some hard work we survived and prospered. Whilst nothing ever goes back to the way it was before, life and business evolve and we all have to face the challenges set before us with a positive attitude.

My first job in sales was with Raleigh Industries when they actually made bicycles and many of the components. I was just nineteen and had been working in London as a van driver delivering relined brake shoes. My prospective boss, a blunt Yorkshire man who loved whiskey and cricket, asked the Sales and Marketing Director if it was acceptable to employ a Minor. He was from a mining town in Derbyshire and replied that it didn't matter what I had done previously, if Bob thought I was right for the job then he wasn't snobbish!

Robert Forsyth taught me that time spent in front of a customer was never wasted and that employing young people is good for business because they go where "Angels fear to tread". He also taught me to listen to the customers needs and translate them into actionable detail, to work hard by putting effort and enthusiasm into tasks and to "think outside the box."

However unlike the banking world he knew when to listen to the voices of experience and managed a progressive balanced team.

When I was a "filthy" smoker I used to love to torment my Mother in Law by inserting little exploding slivers into her opened packets of cigarettes, just a couple in each of her several opened packets. My wife to be, avenged her Mother and herself when I offered a prospective senior buyer at a large wholesale group a cigarette and after a few puffs the end blew off. Though I thought it was hilarious and couldn't stop laughing, I learned to prepare properly for an interview in the future.

Again in my early twenties when I was left in sole charge of our exhibition stand in Frankfurt on the middle weekend of the show and many of the exhibitors had left early on the Saturday I noticed that those Banner people had deserted their post as had Oldham Batteries. I placed all the Banner Batteries on display on the Oldham stand and vice versa. On the Monday morning the Banner personnel were initially shocked, then laughed but the Oldham people were extremely annoyed. I ended up working for Banner and Oldham no longer produce batteries.

Of course I pray for sub zero temperatures in winter and very hot days in the summer which are every batteryman's dream but the reality is that we have to earn our sales. The most important thing to remember is that the customer is King but that the whole package counts.

My advice to young people is to marry only once but wisely, be positive when your glass is only half full, remember that hard work never killed anyone and laughter is the best tonic.

www.bannerbatterien.com

ANTHONY ORMEROD

Company Director

I was MD of newspaper and magazine distribution company covering North Bedfordshire and part of Milton Keynes. We have staff of some 80 in total in the two areas. A 24 hour operation, 7 days a week, 364 days a year – we had Christmas Day off.

My Grandfather started the business, so it was well established when I joined in 1960. During my time we expanded into the then new city of Milton Keynes.

Success was down to attention to detail and keeping the daily distribution well oiled and timely so that the public could buy their newspapers without interruption – a daily challenge. Keeping dedicated and happy staff was key to the operation and a fair amount of time was spent on personnel issues.

We had to do staff appraisals regularly and it was later that I realised no-one was doing an appraisal for me. I had my two Managers do that and it was the best lesson I learned and made me a better boss because I had to address my problem areas as well as everyone else's.

My Mantra
Look for the strengths in the people who work for you, recognising their weaknesses so as to get the best from them.

Funny moments in my career
We did derail a goods train in Bedford station one morning before the rush hour when a barrow loaded with newspapers, its handle came to rest on the track and we watched the goods wagons jumping off the rails. We took statements from all involved ready to deal with the wrath of the rail company but never heard a word from them much to our relief. In those days newspapers came daily by train and we had 3 staff packing orders for individual newsagents ready to send to them by van when they arrived in Bedford – time being the key in order to have them there for the public to buy on their way to work.

My Advice to you
The workplace is a team environment in the main and getting the best from everyone is key. If there is a square peg in a round hole you have to fix it for the wider benefit of the others.

MARK PAGE

Regional Director UK & Ireland for Federal Mogul Aftermarket Ltd

My name is Mark Page I am 39 years of age, my current position is Regional Director UK & Ireland for Federal Mogul Aftermarket Ltd. In this capacity I am responsible for the P & L of the U.K. Aftermarket business that operates from our Regional Distribution Centre located in Bradford.

Federal Mogul are a premier supplier of automotive products, services and solutions to original equipment manufacturers that use our quality components in their vehicles and automotive systems, and to aftermarket customers who sell our world renown brand-name replacement parts through distributors and retail outlets.

It would be fair to say that in my secondary school days I wasn't crystal clear on the career path I wanted to follow. Once I woke up to the fact that even with all the commitment and enthusiasm I placed into a number of individual and team sports at county and in some cases national levels it takes someone really special to achieve professional status. These extremely committed and often selfish individuals deserve the accolades they collect as their dedication can bring isolation from other enjoyable pursuits during hours of physical and mental endurance.

Whilst the professional sportsman path wasn't to be for me I look back now on my days working within a business environment and I genuinely believe a lot of my success and drive is due to the competitive atmosphere I placed myself in, most evenings and weekends participating in sports. It taught me some key attributes: leadership, competitiveness, commitment and team work all of which are relevant in whatever career you embark upon.

My lucky break that kick started me onto a career path that lead me to my position now came whilst competing at a National Swimming gala in Scotland when I was 16. My father always maintained that three key elements often play a part of what happens in your life, after all you can't plan for every eventuality all of the time! 'Timing, luck & knowing someone'!! Whilst taking a break from the pool side after competing I sat with a friend and his father. We spoke for quite sometime on a number of different topics. During the discussion we spoke about my expectations after completing college, at which point he realised that I hadn't figured out all the details as I was focused on the Business Studies course I was studying.

At the time I didn't know it but this social conversation ended up with me getting an interview as a trainee Sales Engineer with an international engineering company. Another thing you learn in life is your peers like to tell you every once in a while 'I told you so' and my father took his chance because this lucky break had all three elements. 1. Timing - the conversation took place when the position was vacant, 2. Luck – I sat down at the right table in the café! 3. Knowing someone who turned to be the Sales Manager looking to recruit.

In the past 23 years working in a Sales Management environment I have encountered many defining moments, I have always tried to take something from each of them whether the situation turned out to be negative or positive. In terms of a career defining moment that I would recall as a huge step and personal goal, was the first time I became top sales person by exceeding business plan target for my territory, fending off challenges from other more experienced and seasoned sales team members. This made me realise that experience and knowledge can carry you so far but there is no replacement for enthusiasm and determination to succeed. This accolade not only brought me some financial benefit which no denying, motivates and stimulates you into more success, but in terms of career development it provided me with additional confidence to believe in myself and my capabilities.

In the business world today people have to be flexible and willing to change strategies in line with market conditions, you have to have a number of management styles to ensure you can obtain the best from your team and ultimately lead your department or organisation towards success. The surroundings you are exposed to at school, college, university, sports teams and general social events are settings that broaden your horizon and develop your proficiency to handle different situations.

In my experience working in a sales management capacity and more recently a general management position, you are only as successful as the team you have around you. Ensuring they perform to your expectations, understanding their strengths and weaknesses, and installing an atmosphere that stimulates the team to succeed are imperative. If your goal is to be a Manager or Director you must be clear in your direction and set realistic but challenging targets, act with integrity but most of all have the ability to listen to others.

My final thoughts for you in whatever route you take on your career path would firstly include setting yourself personal goals and objectives that will challenge you and place you outside of your comfort zone. Secondly, remember 'people buy from people' being completely focused on your goals without taking into account the surroundings and individuals you work with, could hinder rather than help you along the way…

DAVID POTTS

Retail & Logistics Director of Tesco

David Potts is the Retail and Logistics Director of Tesco, the third largest retailer in the world. Tesco employs 300,000 staff in the UK and has 2,114 stores in the UK. David joined Tesco in 1973 and was appointed to the board in 1998.

My First Steps to Success:

I joined Tesco when I was 16. At that time supermarkets were a bit looked down on – people were used to shopping in lots of smaller shops. But I loved it. Working so closely with customers, trying each day to give them a better service than yesterday, working with a great team. It was fantastic. And I still love that chance to be in stores and help customers – when I spot a way to make a customers shopping trip that little bit more enjoyable, I still get a buzz.

When I think back to my first job at Tesco – working on the meat counter in a store in Manchester – the things that were important to me then, still are today. I would get that meat counter looking fantastic and I would talk to customers to find out what they liked and make changes to make my counter look as appealing as possible.

And when I think about what is important to me now – finding out what our customers think, what matters to them, how they shop, how we can make their shopping trip better – they are all as important to me today as when I was on that meat counter. My job may have changed but the things that are important have remained the same.

There have been many highlights during my career. But there are two that stand out for me. One has been seeing all the young people that were working for me in stores when I was a divisional director get on in the business. I and others have helped develop and support them, so that many of them are now in leadership positions themselves. I feel very proud when I see them leading their businesses and moving the firm forward.

The second was when I was asked to go and lead the Irish business we had just bought in 1997. To manage two businesses in two different countries was a great challenge and something I learnt a lot from. Suddenly I had to deliver in a different way and perform at a higher level.

My mantra has always been - you can't do business sat on your butt – sometimes you have a bad day or feel tired. But you can't sit about. You need to get on with it. And I've been fortunate to work for a company that is full of other people with the same approach. We don't like to sit around talking at Tesco If there's one thing I wish I'd known when I was younger – it would be that if I thought something, I would say it out loud. As I've got on, I've realised that if you're thinking something, other people will be too! And if you say it, it will spark ideas for others to contribute to as well. In all my career – no-one has ever turned around to me and said "that was a stupid idea". But I wish I'd realised that a bit earlier, been a bit bolder and pushed my ideas forward more. That would be one piece of advice I'd give to young people starting out in work – don't hold back your ideas.

If you want to do well in retailing – you need to realise that it's important to be happy working with thousands of different people, great people, ordinary people. Retail has one of the most diverse staff groups in business. You need to enjoy serving the public. All of our managers are retailers first and managers second. At Tesco even managers based in our offices spend at least one week a year working in a store – so that they really understand the people at the heart of our business. It is impossible to do well in retail if you don't have that understanding. I think the other thing to say about retailing is that it's a fast paced, dynamic environment and it's a great place to work if you get easily bored. No day is ever the same!

When I think about the future – one of the things I'm very excited about is the energy in the business behind our training. Young people are so important to the future of our business – they are the future leaders. We've always offered people the chance to get on at Tesco and it offers a great career to anyone looking for a chance to work for an international business that moves fast.

We've recently opened a foundation degree in retail – the first of its kind. It fits with our people and their jobs, it is simple and offers the chance for them to learn about the best practice across the industry. It's a great way for our staff to work, study and get the external qualification to back up their practical experience. We also offer A-level Options – our fast track development programme where you join us after sixth form. After 12 months of support and development you are ready to be a manager at the end of it. And we also offer apprenticeships – these are open to everyone but great for young people and offer a nationally recognised qualification awarded by City & Guilds at the end of it.

MARK PRICE

Managing Director of Waitrose

Mark Price was appointed Managing Director, Waitrose in April 2007, and is responsible for the 198 Waitrose shops of the John Lewis Partnership. He joined the Partnership on the Graduate Training Scheme in 1982, before becoming the youngest ever Managing Director of a John Lewis Department Store at High Wycombe and then at John Lewis Cheadle.

Mark transferred to Waitrose in February 1998 as the Partnership's first ever Marketing Director, and in 2000 was additionally given responsibility for retail operations, becoming Director of Selling & Marketing. In another first for the Partnership, Mark was also the youngest individual appointed to the board at that time. Immediately prior to his current role, Mark had been at John Lewis Department Stores since 2005, in the roles Partnership Development Director and John Lewis Development Director.

Mark was also the first supermarket MD to successfully launch a blog - many other business leaders have tried and failed. He blogged for a year to catalogue his attempts lose weight (with moderate success!) and gathered many loyal fans (both customers and Waitrose Partners) along the way. He ended the blog in December2008.
http://www.waitrose.com/blog/

How did you make your first steps to success, and what do you consider to be the key to your success?
I became a John Lewis Partnership graduate trainee and haven't looked back! Having a vision of where I wanted my career to go helped me focus on goals and milestones along the way.
What have been your most valuable career-defining experiences?
Being fortunate to have a great mentor in a John Lewis Director, Brian O'Callaghan, from whom I learned a great deal. Finding a mentor or someone you respect and can model yourself on is hugely beneficial.

What do you wish you had known when you were younger?
The journey is more important than arriving.

Do you have a personal Mantra?
"No guts, no glory!"

Are there any funny / comic moments that you can remember from your career?
I was invited to attend a reception at No. 10 Downing Street and decided to walk from our head office near Victoria train station in London. Along the way I became increasingly desperate for the bathroom and all of the public lavatories around Westminster were closed for some reason. By the time I arrived in Downing Street, I was sweating with stress! As I was introduced to Prime Minister Tony Blair, I could only blurt out "where are the toilets?". It was very embarrassing, but Tony was very gracious and understanding!

What advice would you have for young people just starting out in the world?
Life's much shorter than you think it will be, so enjoy your youth and be happy.

CHRIS REES

President of Volvo Construction Equipment Europe

Business Description:
A division of Volvo AB, a Swedish company manufacturing and distributing construction equipment worldwide.

Job Description:
Responsible for sales, marketing and product support of Volvo Construction Equipment in Europe. I manage a team of some 1700 people throughout Europe.

How did I get started?

Having trained as a lawyer, I realised that my career probably lay in a different direction! After leaving law school, I began working for a construction equipment rental company, firstly as an operator and then as a field engineer. During my vacation time both at school and at university, I had worked in the construction equipment business so this was a natural place to begin my career – I knew that I enjoyed the business and the people that worked in it.

Keys to Success

I joined Volvo as a product support manager, running a service depot in the north of England. I then progressed through the sales department, becoming the head of sales and then Managing Director of the company in Great Britain, before becoming President of the business in Europe. In a large company like Volvo, it is important to put the job first – if you are good, you will progress. Putting yourself before the company rarely leads to success!

Most valuable career defining experiences

Managing through a downturn was probably the most valuable lesson – in the early 1990s, the construction equipment market in Great Britain collapsed just after I had taken over as Managing Director. It was a hard lesson in management, particularly the importance of looking after the cash and proved to be an excellent foundation for running a bigger business in the future.

What do you wish you had known when you were younger ?

Lots of things! The great thing with youth is that there is a natural energy, drive and optimism – when I look back, I do not think that I would have done much differently. A good organisation will always identify and reward talent – I have always managed my career looking forward in 3 year blocks. You should set yourself targets for achievement within that time and if you do not get what you want, make sure that it is not you that is the problem!
My personal mantra
This is very simple – respect. Every person in the organisation deserves respect for the role that they play – an organisation without respect will never reach its full potential.

Funny/comic moments

During a Volvo conference in the north of Scotland, all the delegates were given a Barbour jacket. Before leaving the airport in Scotland, I made sure that my Volvo car keys were safely in the jacket pocket. When I returned to Heathrow, the keys failed to open my car, whilst at the same time my counterpart in France was trying to do the same thing – two Barbour jackets, two sets of Volvo keys, two taxi rides home from the airport!

Advice for young people just starting out in the world of business:

Be good at listening. Most of the mistakes that you will make in your career have been made before and by listening you save a lot of personal stress and cost.

Do not be afraid to make decisions. If you make 10 decisions, you will probably get 2 of them wrong but the other 8 move the business forward – not to make decisions is not to be a business person.
Finally, find a senior person in the organisation who is willing to be your mentor – this should be someone that you respect and trust. I can remember when I was at a junior level in the organisation finding it very difficult to understand the best way forwards – an experienced manager with a willingness to develop talent is a great asset.

The world of business is never boring – there is always a fresh challenge and another opportunity to explore. I still really enjoy my job, which I guess is the best endorsement of all!

STEFFEN SCHIOTTZ-CHRISTENSEN

Chief Executive Officer and Group Vice-President,
Maersk Logistics North Asia

I am a Danish National at 41 years of age and have headed Maersk Logistics in North Asia for the last 8 years. We do shipping and logistic services and have more than 10,000 customers and a turnover of about $750 million employing more than 5,000 people (mostly Chinese.)

The key to my career so far was first a reasonable education – I have a BA from Denmark and I followed it with a 1 year short course in business. After that I considered to go on studying, but decided to get some practical experience instead and opted to work for the A.P Moller – Maersk group as trainee.

The reason for this was simply curiosity and a desire to travel, knowing that Maersk is a global company, I was very attracted to it and in addition to the fact that Maersk is the most famous and prestigious company in Denmark.

I clearly feel that this was a key defining moment towards my first steps of a successful professional career. The learning point early on for me was:

Education is good, but it is what you use it for that matters – you can be as educated as anybody, but you must get out in real life and do real business early on and gain some practical experience. Also learn that money does not come for free and you need to work to make it and save to keep it.

You learn and study life long – I went back to school at 35 and got an MBA from IMD in Switzerland.

In terms of career defining moments it was my early decision to go abroad at age 22 and leave my family, girl-friend behind and my life as I knew it. The experience to live in United States alone and learn how to manage my own life and job prepared me well for future challenges. It was always my dream to be a global citizen and I have never looked back and have been outside Denmark for 20 years now to Africa, USA, Philippines, Japan, Thailand and China. The points here are:

Be curious – you have a lot of life ahead of you and use it to the fullest – you only live once.

Pursue your dreams and make sacrifices to get there

When looking back at my career, I wish I had realized much earlier that people and the team is everything.

You can be a very bright and outgoing person and believe that you can personally fix and manage everything, but that is not the always the case. You need to lead and manage a team and be a trust worthy leader, or you will not achieve your goals.

So: Team and people first – everyone has different qualities and it is your obligation to get the best out of people and treat all of them with basic respect. The team is only as good as the weakest player and it is your obligation to help and coach the weakest link – so ensure success for team and yourself.

I do not really have a personal mantra as such, but living optimistically – the glass is always half full....
You do not have problems – you have opportunities and challenges! Something bad can always turn into something good.

One of the funniest things I have experienced in my long career was my first sales call on a client in the Philippines. I knew absolutely nothing about the client or the business and managed an hour of the call without any knowledge or preparation. The client never knew or realised my complete lack of business knowledge and even appreciated the attention!

You can manage a lot of things without preparation and by impulse or "gut-feeling", but you need to follow-up on such experiences and learn from them.

My advice to young people is to get out there – fast – the world is yours to conquer and do not hold back. Use your youthful energy and passion to pursue your own dreams and make this a better place for all of us.

Good luck to you all!

TODD STITZER

What drives you, what motivates you?
I love to accomplish things. I had two great parents who always challenged me to do the best that I could do in a broad range of things.

Who is your inspiration in life?
My father, a YMCA director, and my mother a nurse, were always incredibly focused on education, accomplishment, doing things for others, and they did great things for their kids.

Tell me a bit more about your leadership style?
My leadership style is inclusive, it is focused and it is energetic. I think it is really important that you seek to be as egoless as you possibly can. You want people who have a team orientation but an accomplishment orientation.

Why Cadbury? Why not CEO of any other big multinational?
I found the culture to be highly consistent with my own values. People were incredibly friendly; they had huge integrity and respect for their colleagues. People who work at Cadbury think it is such a great place, because they have found such an incredible group of kindred souls. Respect for other people, integrity, winning on a team, all those things are core moral-fibre values for everybody.

What does being the biggest and best mean?
Being the best means having a balanced but very high set of standards from a commercial perspective, from a financial perspective, from a cultural and behavioural perspective. It means that very elusive sort of standard of doing it all really, really well. It means having great advertising; it means having a great balance sheet; it means having a social connection to our communities, both our employee community and our external communities that is respected and loved. It is this sense of multi-dimensional excellence.

What are the key consumer trends that you have noticed and how is Cadbury equipped to deal with them?
Consumers absolutely want quality products, things that taste good, that look good, that they can get for good value. We always, always have to be sure that our products are high quality and good value. Consumers want to feel that the way in which we manufacture, procure and create our products is sustainable. We have sought as a company, through the Cadbury Cocoa Partnership (our cocoa sustainability programme), through our Purple Goes Green programme, to respond to environmental and social needs in a way that relates directly to our manufacturing processes, our supply chain.

What are the markets that you think would be interesting for Cadbury in the future?
30% of our business comes from emerging markets, and it is a great strength. Greater investment for us in places like Latin America, Africa, Asia and India is crucial.

What about diversity in the workplace?
Diversity is crucial. You need the best mix of people - people from different places, and people with different perspectives. Having the right mix of ideas, people and backgrounds gets you a better business.

What advice would you give somebody who is just starting off their corporate career?
Firstly, find a place that you love. Secondly, hopefully that place will satisfy your own curiosity, intellectually and professionally, by allowing you to move through different experiences. If you want to be successful in the greater business world today, it is getting increasingly global, so you need to show that you are able to deal with multiple cultures, in multiple functions, in multiple geographies.

Is it possible for a business to be competitive and capitalist on one hand, and caring on the other, or do the two conflict in some way?

I do not think they conflict, but it makes you work harder. You have to be more thoughtful, and you have to work a bit harder to come up with a dynamic that is both shareowner friendly, and community friendly. It can be done and Cadbury has done it for a long time – nearly 200 years.

Cadbury made a substantial investment in to the Cadbury Cocoa Partnership, £45 million, why is that?

The rationale is that cocoa is one of our principle ingredients in the business that is the biggest business we have. If we do not come up with a way to help the people who grow our cocoa feel as if it is a great occupation, that is it worthwhile, that it is healthy, that it is something to be handed down to the next generation, then we run the risk of not having enough ingredients for the main product that we sell. We created the cocoa industry in Ghana in 1908, we have a responsibility to keep that industry sustainable, and, again, it is the symbiotic thing. We need cocoa, but we also need it to be created in a sustainable way that is sustainable both for the earth and for the people who farm it.

You are taking more of a leadership role in terms of Purple Goes Green, more than other manufacturing companies. Is there any particular reason behind that?

It is a programme that works both ways. It helps the environment and it helps Cadbury save money. We get the good feeling of treating the environment with care, and we get the good business result that we generally save money, because we are using less water, electricity, and heat.

If you had to sum up Cadbury's future in three words, what would they be?

Biggest and best.

ANDY STREET

Managing Director of John Lewis

Profession/short job description:
I am responsible for all activities within the John Lewis Division of the Partnership. The other "Division" is Waitrose. So my job includes the shops, on-line, distribution and head office activities.

How did you make your first steps to success, and what do you consider to be the key to your success?
First steps - I joined John Lewis on the graduate training scheme, spending my first year working on the shop floor at John Lewis Brent Cross. My key to success - having great mentors in the organisation. Watch and learn from them.

What have been your most valuable career-defining experiences?
Getting something badly wrong. When I was Supply Chain Director, big changes went wrong and cost us a lot of money. However my boss at the time supported me and we pressed on with the changes and learnt from them. Everyone should learn from failures.

What do you wish you had known when you were younger?
To listen more. there is always pressure to "perform" oneself - but the best of leaders let others perform. They listen well to take the few big decisions correctly.

Do you have a personal Mantra?
Mantra - in career planning - look after the present and the future will look after itself. Too many people are so obsessed with their next job that they fail to attend to the current one. That's fatal.

Are there any funny / comic moments that you can remember from your career?
Not really comic, but interesting. After leaving university I started work as a selling assistant. A number of university colleagues came into the shop, saw me and asked if I had failed my finals. How wrong they were. In truth a good leader needs to understand and appreciate the roles of the junior members of the team; they are critical to success.

What advice would you have for young people just starting out in the world?
Above all else, do something you enjoy. Don't worry about the career paths, salaries and all of that. Work is a marathon - so be sure you enjoy the early paces.

MIKE THOMPSON

Managing Director of Weblight

Profession/ short job description:
Initially trained as a chartered accountant, but 14 years ago I set up and internal lighting maintenance company servicing retail clients across the country. I still run this as MD.

How did you make your first steps to success and what do you consider to be the key to your success?
The first stage in any success I may have had was to obtain a training contract with what was considered to be the top firm of accountants in London. I worked with a peer group of people, many of whom have left me standing in terms of their achievements and several of whom are now household names, but to work in that environment is stimulating and challenging.

Secondly you need to find the environment that suits you as an individual. I worked abroad in a senior position for Shell early in my career and realised that I could never work in the shifting environment that was Shell head office in London and started to look for my future roles in smaller businesses. However, it was important to know from experience that this was the case.

What have been your most valuable career defining experiences?
I think you tend to learn faster and more enduringly from mistakes, rather than from success. The secret must be to push the boundaries, but not to go too far!

I was finance director for 3 years in a computer systems company in Cambridge that was a world leader in satellite image interpretation (winning the Queen's Award for Technology). The problem was that at the price we had to sell the systems in the early '90s, the only markets were the military and a limited academic community. This was insufficient to sustain the growth of the business and so it had to be swallowed up into one of the 2 large American competitors. With the massive increase in computer power, you can now get most of the functionality we were producing when you download Google Earth (and for free!). We had great technology, but no practical market. The lesson is to check the market wants what you have.

What do you wish you had known when you were younger?
So much of importance comes from experience and one has to go through life to gain it! However, I wish I had understood people better when I was younger; I was arrogant and over confident and could never understand why many people did not share my priorities in life and show the same commitment to things that I felt I did. In reality you cannot run a successful business without a good team. A good team needs a balance of all sorts of people and you actually need (and must not abuse) people with priorities in other areas so that they can carry out what may seem to be mind numbingly boring tasks accurately and reliably and achieve satisfaction through this.

Success in a business is down to teamwork and it takes all sorts of different types of people to achieve that. This does not mean that you do not have to remove and change members of the team from time to time, but not respect people who are loyal and effective simply because they do not share your values is the quick route to a failing team.

What advice would you have for young people just starting out in the world of business?
Unless you have an over-riding certainty of what you mean to do, do not restrict yourself too early. Make sure your experience is as broad as possible, but always of the best quality. Working abroad can be a great learning experience and is probably best done young without the ties of children.

Is there anything else that you would like to add?
When you are head of a team, make sure you understand what each of the members is going through by experiencing as much of their job as possible. At Tesco, the main board goes onto the shop floor for at least one week a year and I have done night shift work with my guys changing lamps in a supermarket. Never be afraid to start at, or go back to the bottom.

"
I wish I'd known how little I knew.
But that's a cliché.
"

John Moule

Education

Education

Teaching is an incredibly rewarding and highly important job. Ultimately educators teach others and share their vast wealth of knowledge in order to provide them with the necessary skills for life. It would be wrong to suggest that educators are always highly remunerated financially but job satisfaction can be high, encouraging others to learn more about the world around them.

Exam success is major objective to demonstrate that teachers have fulfilled the requirements of the curriculum, but there is much more to teaching than simply tests and assessments. Teachers are there to teach the vital life skills that we will hold dear to us whatever career path we choose to follow. When teaching young children up to the age of 13, many teachers teach a host of subjects but as the students get older, especially at upper school, teachers become specialised. The latter is the case for university lecturers, often the most knowledgeable people in their field of expertise.

JAMES FOWLER

Headmaster of Aldenham School

"I didn't get where I am today…"

To draw out some succinct advice for anyone setting out on a career in the early 21st century is a task that almost certainly requires the wisdom of Solomon, but in my current role as a Headmaster, responsible for shaping the education of 550 pupils aged between 11 and 18 I should presumably have something to offer.

But, it was never intended to be like this. My career has been marked by a willingness to follow passions and enthusiasms, not a pre-planned job path. Yet this willingness to be responsive and thereby to change and develop is almost certainly the facet of my life that has been most influential in my career. I very much doubt that I would have reached where I am now by simply following a linear career path. That is not to say that I am an especially bold or brave person in other areas of my life, but in terms of the way I spend over half my waking hours for each day of the week I have always had to be certain that I was enjoying myself. And sometimes that has meant change, flexibility and a willingness to try something new.

I suspect that the ISCO careers advisor was having a quiet laugh behind his teacup as he suggested that the career for me was to be a surveyor, since anyone with less practical sense, or spatial awareness would be hard to imagine. So, not for the first time in my life, I ignored his advice and chose A Level courses that interested me – and suddenly school was much more enjoyable as a result. Likewise I was determined that my time at Oxford was to give me the chance to do as much singing and performing as possible, whilst making sure that my Theology degree was kept on course. That took me to perform all over Europe in concert halls, churches and on opera stages, but I was fairly sure that this was not going to be for me the career path that would give me a life I would enjoy.

So instead, straight after university when everyone around me was insistent that the thing that would be most important in their workplace was the company of graduates I began work on a local newspaper in the advertising sales office where I was the only graduate – such places were still common in the early 1980s. I was not the only young man trying to make his living there whilst his mind was on the future, since the message boy in the office was a certain Steve Redgrave who was just beginning training for his second Olympic gold medal!

The crucial thing that I learned straightaway was that my qualifications were not going to sell advertising space – I was. And I was perfectly willing to approach anyone to do so. I do recall that my experience of selling extremely successful features on independent schools and pulling the wool over the eyes of the bursars in those schools may have been a sign of things to come.

Yet when I needed to move on to London and the highly competitive world of advertising agencies a year later, my education and contacts from Oxford were very useful. As indeed they were as I started to deal with clients in a whole host of blue chip companies. These were generally people old enough to be my mother or father, and I can only imagine how young, callow and inexperienced I must have seemed, but a little conviction in getting your presentation together went a very long way. The fact that I was in no way a visually creative person didn't seem to matter if I could get the creative teams to perform to the best of their abilities. And hence the management and inspiration of others became a skill and a passion. The structure of an advertising agency is built, like so many businesses, around teams and it is certainly a great way to work.

Eventually however my frustration with being at the behest of the clients meant that the glamour of advertising wore off. If you are considering any career in a client service capacity think carefully about the fact that the client (or possibly his wife) is always right!

And then, as so often in my life, I met a mentor who would allow me to change direction. I can certainly confirm that my career has been built on a series of meetings with people whose faith in me allowed them to trust me with increasing amounts of responsibility and to whom I owe a great deal. Everyone will meet these people in their lives and the key to happiness is in being open to their suggestions and ideas. Not many people will have a meeting as I did with someone who will persuade them to take on a new career at the age of 29 for which they had no direct training, meant that they had to give in their company car, and take a significant drop in salary with no guarantee of success. But something in that meeting with the first headmaster I worked for convinced me that all this would be worth it. And once the decision was made and I began teaching I knew that this was my life's work.

The remarkable autonomy that the classroom teacher enjoys to shape the children in their care is a fabulous, if daunting, opportunity and I am always thrilled to see new teachers get the same enjoyment. But for me, the life of the school extended far beyond the classroom and I was quickly running sports teams, leading two departments, directing school plays and musicals and taking children on skiing trips. For me, once I had found my true vocation I knew that I would commit fully and then progress.

And from there on I knew that I would not only spend my working life in schools, but that I wanted to lead them and ensure that they were as effective as possible. Hence, the beginning of my quest to become a headmaster and a determined career path of promotion and development. Such a course is entirely plausible once you know where you are headed and for me it led to me becoming Headmaster of Aldenham School by the age of 43. Each day is marked by variety, unpredictable events and the chance to share your thoughts and vision with others – what an extraordinary privilege. Of course other jobs have the same features, but for me nothing could be as enjoyable – so far….

JOHN MOULE

Headmaster of Bedford School (1100 boys aged 7-18)

In many ways, I have never really planned a career. I fell into teaching and had little intention of doing it for more than a few years. I stayed. I never really planned promotion either but things just came at the right time. The key is probably just a mixture of being good at what I do and getting bored easily so looking for the next challenge . . . and enjoying the job too. I have always loved my job . . . almost always.

Career defining experiences come along, on occasion, but more important are career defining people: the first Deputy Head I worked with who taught me the old fashioned art of school-mastering, the first head I worked with who told me I should be a head in the future. If there's one thing that really matters, it's recognizing how valuable people are in your life. Take advice and remember it even when you don't take it – it'll come in handy later. I don't believe in personal mantras particularly but the philosophy I have adopted is 'care but don't care too much' ie put your heart and soul into what you do but don't lose sleep at night over it.

And remember to laugh at yourself at the time or after the event: when I fell over a bench after midnight and knocked myself out at my previous school; the frightening and surreal experience of a boy in my boarding house running away to attempt to join up with the Taliban in Afghanistan and him being picked up by Interpol on a known drugs trafficking route in Slovenia; and of picking a shaving cut two minutes before my first staff meeting as Head and so having to conduct the meeting with blood pouring from my face.

Oh, and my teaching career nearly ended fairly soon after it started when I called a girl 'a stupid cow' in a rash moment. The Deputy head referred to the above, took me aside and admonished me . . . having done so, he smiled laconically and said: 'stupid bag would have been better'. Great man.

My advice would be to learn early the value of recognising one's own ignorance. Of realising how much one will regret wasting time at university. Of appreciating that it is always worth listening but always worth standing up for what you believe in too. Of believing in things. Of being laid-back. Of being grateful for what we can be grateful for.

And what do I wish I had known? Not sure really. That's the phlegmatic coming through. I wish I'd known how little I knew. But that's a cliché. I wish I 'd known that teachers are not just objects to make fun of. But that's a cliché too, especially from a Head Master. I wish I'd known how to bat properly. But I still don't. I wish, I suppose, I'd known what it is to have the drive to succeed a little earlier: times and opportunities sometimes only come round once. Cliché again? I wish I'd known how often clichés are true.

www.bedfordschool.org.uk

Dr. Richard Palmer

Teacher, Author & Consultant

Profession/short job description:
I've been a full-time secondary teacher for thirty-five years (English, Theatre Studies, Classical Civilisation, Study Skills and Critical Thinking). Author of eighteen books; Open University Tutor for over a decade; ISI Inspector since 1985; Educational Consultant and Jazz Critic.

How did you make your first steps to success, and what do you consider to be the key to your success?
I'm not sure I'd call myself 'a success': I'm still hungrily looking for that. But I've had a fortunately varied and enriching professional life, and I suppose it began in my L6 year. I had intended to be a linguist (French & German), but at 16 I had the most wonderful English teacher (Raymond Wilson)who changed my life. He not only within a few weeks led to me to opt for English beyond school; he taught me the importance of humour, of true as opposed to assumed scholarship, of how teaching is essentially a matter of joyous sharing with the young while having a very good time yourself - and learning from your charges.

What have been your most valuable career-defining experiences?
One I've cited already - that marvellous 6th form teacher. Although on graduation I initially wanted to be a University Lecturer, I think it was my memory of his lessons as well as my pleasure in being with the young that made me plump, happily, for secondary teaching. I was of course fortunate, in that getting the aforementioned Open University contract gave me the best of both worlds, but I'd never have switched sectors on a full-time basis. Second: discovering jazz at the age of seventeen in 1964. I did so initially in desperation: I seemed to be the only person in the entire Western Hemisphere who couldn't stick The Beatles at any price (I still can't), and I looked for something else to listen to. That not only led to the greatest love of my life, and thirty years as a jazz critic (1500+ reviews and a many articles), but also eventually meant that I met the great Oscar Peterson, becoming his close friend and, climactically, engaged as Editor & Consultant on his 2001 autobiography. I've recently been afforded the similarly privileged commission by the composer, arranger and magnificent musician Lalo Schifrin. You may not know the name, but I'm sure you know Mission Impossible, Bullitt, Dirty Harry and The Three Tenors: all his work, and it was wonderful to collaborate with him. Third, and finally: the (early) realisation that I did not want to be a Housemaster, let alone a Headmaster. I've worked for and with many excellent such bosses, so don't think I'm denigrating those posts or the people who occupy them. But I treasure my Sundays and my evenings, when I can work at my own stuff or, more simply, not be 'on call'. I believe that the private work I have done - my books, my external teaching and consultancies – have not only given me pleasure and remuneration but made me a better teacher: the separate activities feed each other and make each one more satisfying and, I hope, more enabling for my various students. That's what primarily matters to me: being 'in power' does not.

What do you wish you had known when you were younger?
I hope this does not sound smug or conceited, but it's not so much a question of 'What I wish I had known' as 'What I wish I had done'. I reckon that in a dim, uncodified way, by the time I was sixteen I knew most of what was important: love; the need for dedication, whatever it is you are dedicated to; that people are so much more important than systems or organisations; that, in the late Sir Kingsley Amis's unimprovable words, '80% of everything is crap'. (The secret, of course, is to discern and treasure the remaining 20%.) I wish I'd worked harder at playing the piano. I was good, but not good enough: I wasn't properly serious about it. I wish I'd not been such an abject moron when it came to science; maybe I wasn't all that well taught - I'd have loved to have been taught Chemistry and Physics by some of the people who've been my adult colleagues - but part of the problem was that my time as a schoolboy was ferociously compartmentalised. I knew that at 12 I would be able to drop several subjects because I was already designated 'a linguist', and that meant I turned off pretty early from those disposable disciplines. And while I've arduously attempted to educate myself in those dropped subjects, I don't think the system that defined my schooldays was all that bright. Finally: I wish that I hadn't at times been such a coward, or 'sensible', about things that enraged me. Yes, choose your moments with care, and don't explode too often; but there comes a time when you have to 'say a word or two', and I sometimes think I haven't done that often enough.

Do you have a personal Mantra?

Absolutely not. As my pupils will (probably wearily) confirm, there are many wise quotations and observations by all and sundry which I remember and try to act on, but the notion of reducing a complex, often contradictory and always challenging personal existence to a single-concept bromide (Men Are From Mars, Women From Venus/Look For The Real Person Inside Yourself, so on and so endlessly forth) strikes me as both cretinous and posturingly bogus. Your question is a legitimate and topical one, so I don't in the least blame you for it; on the other hand, it is nastily redolent of the sound-bite obsession which I think is one of the worst things about our current culture. All that said, if I were under physical duress to nominate, I'd go for: 'Just shut up and do it.'

Are there any funny / comic moments that you can remember from your career?

Yes - so many that I could fill this book with them. But when outlined for readers who weren't there when such moments occurred, virtually all of them would suffer from being (and forgive this esoteric, academic term) 'not very funny'. However, let me now add that I consider humour not only one of the greatest pleasures in life, but also one of its most important – and seriously instructive - properties. And it is much misunderstood. That great poet Philip Larkin (an enormously funny man, and as it happens also much misunderstood, as I have argued in a recent book) once observed, with mordant wisdom: ''One uses humour to make people laugh. The trouble is, it makes them think you aren't serious. That's the risk you take.' Yea, verily, yea.

The Latin noun gravitas may not spring to everyone's lips, but most of those who do use it get it wrong: they think it means solemnity (i.e. middle-aged pomposity), where in fact it means authority or weight: it is a Galilean/gravitational term, not a Gradgrindian one. Of course, there are occasions when levity is not a good idea, however well-meant: I learnt - slowly and painfully - that committees are one such, and another is the UCAS form that many readers will be engaged upon as I write. But humour, lightness of touch, and a warm delight in life's absurdities as well as its deepest verities are not only essential to sanity but a passport to enablement and true achievement. One more thought on this. It never ceases to depress me that school magazines - any school, any era, any format - have never in my experience even begun to capture what the school in question is actually like on a day-to-day basis. That is, at least partly, because they are not remotely funny: they are earnest almanacs which may well record in exhaustive (and to any outsider, incomprehensible) detail all that the institution has accomplished over the period concerned, but they don't begin to capture the ethos, life and sense of fun that not only underscores all those accomplishments but makes them possible in the first place.

What advice would you have for young people just starting out in the world?

Don't let anybody bully, coerce or even lovingly advise you what to do with your life. There are two things about which you must be utterly selfish: marriage, and what you want to do in terms of your career. If you undertake either to please someone else rather than yourself, it will be a failure, if not a disaster. Make your own mistakes - God knows, we all do - but make them your mistakes, not those of others by proxy.

Is there anything else that you would like to add?

Two things. One: Do not think you must make a life-binding career-choice in your late teens or even early twenties. Things are so much more fluid now for young professionals, and that is wonderful. Just do what you most like, and go on following that principle, even - well, especially - if what it is
you most like changes. Two: my congratulations to all of you who have accomplished this enterprise. I could not have dreamed of doing such a thing at seventeen, and I am sure that is true of virtually all my contemporaries. A signal achievement.

Be positive, never give up.

Micheal Cox

Finance

Finance

The world of finance is a vast one, which encompasses everything from stockbrokers to accountants. Personal financial advisors concentrate on offering individuals investment advice whilst investment bankers are involved in complicated commercial transactions. The reputation of the Banking and Finance sector has suffered recently, but without money the economy would grind to a halt.

It is wrong to think that the only way to get into the world of finance is to do a degree in economics, maths or accounting. Large accounting firms and banks offer a good training programme for school leavers.

GRAHAM BEALE

Chief Executive of Nationwide Building Society

Graham Beale is the Chief Executive of Nationwide Building Society, the world's largest building society. The group has almost 15 million customers, more than £120billion in retail deposits and assets of nearly £200billion. It is the UK's second largest savings provider and third largest mortgage lender.

Nationwide Building Society is a mutual organisation which means it is owned by its members, both borrowers and savers.

Career Journey

"I studied for a degree in psychology at university, and initially planned to pursue a career in marketing. Events were to take a different course and opportunities arose which led to me taking a completely different route into the world of finance. As a result, from an early age I have understood that there is more than one route to achieving your goals. It pays to regard change as an opportunity and to always be flexible and positive in your outlook.

Good qualifications are important. They will give you a head start over others, and will also prove to prospective employers that you are capable of operating at a certain level. Personally for me, a professional accountancy qualification following my degree was an excellent opportunity to build a bridge between an academic and professional working life.

As an ambitious new graduate recruit, it soon became apparent to me that that you must continually prove yourself to progress within any organisation. You must be prepared to work hard and be prepared to undertake some pretty menial work at times. This has stood me in good stead for some of the many challenges I have faced in my career to date. It is important to approach new opportunities with an open mind and an optimistic outlook and to be fleet of foot in adapting to new challenges and new working environments quickly.

When planning my career path I paid particular attention to a horizon of 18-24 months ahead, whilst always maintaining focus on long-term goals. This approach enabled me to drive forward the businesses I ran whilst not losing sight of the bigger picture.

A combination of hard work, knowledge and experience has certainly led to a successful career to date.

I put this success down to a number of key factors:

- **Be clear on what you want to achieve;** set clear objectives and seize every opportunity. If you turn down too many chances, you'll soon build a reputation for yourself and will inevitably miss a golden nugget of opportunity. At some points this may mean taking a step back to take two forwards, or may mean some pressure or imbalance to your work/life routine.
- **Be brave and be prepared to challenge the status quo,** even if it isn't the solution or answer people are hoping for. During the early recession in the 80s/90s I became known as a problem solver and fixer by recognising some of our issues, but also proposing some appropriate solutions. Highlighting a problem area may not always feel like a good idea, but presenting an appropriate solution can demonstrate real leadership and clearly evidence that you are taking responsibility.
- **Be prepared to take risks**, but make sure they are measured and within defined boundaries. It is very important to take some risks along the path to success, but they must be appropriate and balanced and shouldn't move your business beyond its capacity.
- **Be accountable**; lead from the front, listen to the wisdom of the team around you, act decisively and appropriately and learn from your mistakes. No-one is infallible and sometimes our failures can teach us more than our successes. A management consultant once said "reflect and learn from your mistakes and then put them on the wave behind you."

- **Be prepared to compromise;** know your own strengths and limitations and be prepared to listen to or defer to a more experienced view. This is particularly relevant as you move into more senior roles and will not only help you to solve problems creatively, but will also help to build a strong management team.
- **And finally – embrace luck;** we will all have some in our careers and opportunities may come from unexpected sources. A four year secondment improving performance at a subsidiary in Scotland was a key example for me. Uprooting my family and moving away from our head office did not at first appear to be the best career move for me. But it gave me an opportunity, as Managing Director, to lead an important business. This is an experience I can still draw from 12 years later.

High standards and strong personal ethics are really important to me and are key reasons why my career has been successful. Working to these standards has meant that we, as an organisation, have achieved strong results in sometimes difficult times and has helped to underpin and truly establish our mutual business model."

MICHAEL COX

Director of Business Development,
Henderson Global Investors

I spent my career in the City of London working with investors in shares and bonds, the last 16 years of which was for a large international investment management company working within their marketing department where I specialised in the development of new business.

I left school with below average A-levels, partly because I had spent too much time enjoying my sport and other non-academic pastimes! I had no specific ideas on a long term career but wanted to get either a degree or qualification partly to learn more but also in order to get into the top 20% of the workforce academically and therefore improve my chances with potential employers.

I had done Maths at A-level and had managed to gain a place at University to study it further, however I did not really enjoy advanced maths and so decided at the last minute to train as an accountant instead. I did not intend to pursue a career as an accountant but knew that the qualification was in great demand by employers seeking people across their company who had a broad financial and economic understanding, being a key part of any business. Today I might have tried a Business Studies degree, which was not easily available then, as a similar entry to the business world.

I therefore trained as an accountant intending to use the qualification as my `degree substitute`, but additionally it gave me a brief look at a huge variety of different businesses, from media to oil, as I carried out their annual financial audits. This period also made me finally realise that I did not just want to be a company accountant, however well rewarded, as I needed a broader interest!

However I had worked with an investment management company during this training and had really enjoyed the people and what they did, so as soon as I qualified I applied for a job as a salesman in a large firm of stockbrokers in London. They already had very clever academic researchers with some exciting investment ideas and they wanted sales people who understood the ideas but additionally and most importantly had good interpersonal skills so could better articulate these ideas to potential investors, the investment management companies.

The firm of stockbrokers wanted to hire six accountants for these sales roles and I was lucky as there were only some 10 applicants – 10 years later I was running the sales team, interviewing for such roles and there were probably 20 applicants per job as by then the excitement and high rewards were so well publicised! However these excessive profits and rewards for both the stock broking companies and their employees eventually brought about their downfall as over time it attracted too many new companies, too many people and thus too much competition. Like the retail industry today, when an economic slowdown came along there were far too many businesses chasing the customers, so significant closures and redundancies quickly followed.

There are tremendous opportunities in every business for people with good interpersonal skills, people who can explain something simply in a way that outsiders can understand and believe. They can sell, market or represent their company to the outside world and they can make all the difference to the company's success in a competitive marketplace. They are not necessarily the cleverest people in the firm, but they are some of the most valuable and therefore best paid!

Do not be afraid to change your career – and redundancy can be a blessing, even career defining. Businesses and industries evolve very quickly these days and good businesses / industries can, surprisingly, go terminally bad over time. It is no bad thing during one's long working life to reassess earlier plans as new opportunities come along which are sometimes more invigorating and successful going forward.

Be positive, never give up.

My current firm closed our whole division and I was redundant – it was a shock but in hindsight a blessing. I knew my industry was now overstaffed, that the atmosphere was always competitively aggressive and that my job had become less fun, all so different to when I started 20 years earlier. Yet the parallel industry of my investors, the investment management companies, had none of these characteristics. Redundancy gave me the opportunity to review my career and in consequence I moved to an investment management company where my skills were compatible but the industry was immature and opportunities were so much greater.

Over my career, I wish had realised sooner the following key lessons:

Work for a business that you eventually find interesting and exciting. While you will obviously enjoy it more, you will also more likely come up with good ideas internally and will more likely enthuse about it externally - both are excellent for the business and for one's progress!

A degree or qualification is vital to get to an interview for a good job; otherwise you must work up from the bottom.

A commercial or vocational degree was advantageous versus a non-vocational degree. My much brighter school friends had graduated with 1st's in Classics, English Literature etc but found it much harder to get a well paid exciting job than I did with my more practical qualifications!

Speaking with friends and contacts, however distant, discovered potential new jobs before they were advertised or were in the open market

Any interview needed 100%preparation in order to be more impressive than the competition – full knowledge of the company; answers to the 10 most likely questions; a couple of questions about the job or employer e.t.c.

PAULINE LEWIS

Accountant

Profession/ short job description:

I am an Accountant, but more specifically a financial controller of a building and construction company.

How did you make your first steps to success, and what do you consider to be the key to your success?

I took a degree in computing which had Accounting as part of the course so therefore I had the choice after university of what I would prefer to do. In my opinion it is always good to have something else to fall back on in case things don't work out. It is a good idea to have a degree under your belt.

What have been your most valuable career – defining experiences?

To be adaptable! I was offered a position in a software house – unfortunately my work permit at that time did not allow the company to employ me. This is when I went into accountancy and did more training and studying in order to obtain a profession. Nothing is ever wasted in that; all experience is an education towards something else in life.

What do you wish you had known when you were younger?

I wish I had a broader knowledge of the different types of companies – big and small. Small companies enable you to have experience all round, but larger companies have a more structured way of training.

What advice would you have for young people starting out in the world of business?

To start from the bottom is a means of being a good manager when you get to the top.

Is there anything you would like to add?

Enjoy what you want to do. Life would be pretty miserable if you do not enjoy what you do – after all a large percentage of your time in the future will be taken up at work.

STEVE WILLIAMS

Director, Service Quality, Santander UK

What is your role, your responsibility and general background?

I am the Human Resources Director for Abbey, part of the Santander Banking Group.
My overriding aim is to improve the performance and capability of our people and to
support our objective to be the best Commercial Bank in the UK. I want to help our people to be the very best they
can be.

I have 28 great years of experience in Retail Financial Services in the UK, mostly with Barclays but for the last four
years with Banco Santander and Abbey. My background is in Branches, Marketing and Risk. I have been Risk
Director for Barclaycard and Group Fraud Director for Barclays Group. I joined Abbey in 2005 and worked for 3 years
as Risk Director but moved across to become HR Director in January 2008.

How did you make your first steps to success, and what do you consider to be the key to your success?

I was lucky to be awarded an all round scholarship to Millfield School in Street, Somerset and this gave me
academic, sporting and social opportunities to develop such that I then won a scholarship to Pembroke College
Oxford.

The key to my success is luck. Luck was once defined by Seneca, a Roman Philosopher, as the coming together
of preparation and opportunity. I have always been prepared, even from my early days as a Boy Scout with their
motto "Be Prepared". So when the opportunity comes along, I have been ready to take advantage of it.

Gary Player, the golfer was once asked about what made him successful and was it just about being lucky. He
responded "You know I am lucky, and the harder I practice, the luckier I get". This is as true for me, as it was for
him. The harder I have worked, the more I have prepared, the more successful I have been.

What have been your most valuable career-defining experiences?

I have three particular experiences which, although not life or career defining, were very important to me.

Experience 1 - In my mid to late twenties whilst still at Barclays, I did not move on as quickly as one or two peers
whom I considered to be not as good as me. As a result, my attention wandered to a new opportunity and "greener
grass" with TSB Trustcard. Within 3 months I knew that that the grass was not greener and that I had made a
mistake. I plucked up the courage to go back to Barclays and admitted I had made a mistake. After serving some
time as re-entry into Barclays in the Marketing Department, my career started to blossom again and I became
Marketing Manager for Home Mortgages, Personal Lending and Bank Charges and subsequently Area Director of
North Kent.

My learning – never be afraid to admit to being wrong. It is far worse to keep pretending that one is right.

Experience 2 - In the middle of the last Recession in the early 1990s, I was Branch Manager of the largest Retail
Banking Branch in Barclays, South East Region. I was working late as we had lots of paperwork particularly
relating to reporting on customers who were in financial difficulties. A colleague was also working late. I wandered
across and asked what he was doing. He was compiling a Report for the Regional Sports & Social Committee on
our Branch PC. We swapped notes and he showed me how I could use PC programs to automate a lot of the
paperwork we had in branch. Within 1 year we had the best automated Management Information of any Branch in
Barclays covering Sales Management, Customer Service Management, Cost Management, Risk Management and
most importantly People Management. We also used PC screen shows and Desktop Publishing to communicate
factual information in an attention grabbing way. We won the Barclays Operational Branch of the Year Award in
1992.

My learning – "Well presented facts speaker louder than words". Make sure you set your self up for success by having accurate, timely and meaningful management information available to you.

Experience 3 - I was lucky enough to be chosen whilst at Barclays to undertake a Management of Business Administration MBA course at Henley Management College. We had a presentational skills course run by a retired vicar. He said many vicars are poor communicators. They have the best product in the world – everlasting life – but they are selling it to fewer and fewer people.

Every lesson, whether looking at verbal or written communications, he used to stop us and challenge… What's the story? And, what three things do you want me to take away? And he was absolutely insistent upon structure; "tell them what you are going to tell them, sell them what you want to sell them, tell them what you have just told them".

My learning – Be clear and concise on what your key messages are, three at most, and use repetition to make sure your messages stick.

What do you wish you had known when you were younger?

I wish I had known how valuable it is to have excellent linguistic skills to be able to converse and do business in other languages. If I had had the chance again, I would have liked to have spent more time learning other languages. This would involve languages such as German and Spanish, both of which I have dabbled with in later years. I also wish I had learned the piano or guitar, and played for Manchester United but then again….

Do you have a personal Mantra?

My often repeated personal mantra at work is… "I like to achieve things despite, rather than not achieve things because". I find too many people spend too much time and negative energy on what they can't do instead of focusing on what they can do. "Do Something" rather than "Do Nothing".

Are there any funny / comic moments that you can remember from your career?

The time I looked across a very wide staff room in a branch in the Medway Towns and said "I really believe you, Samantha" only to be told afterwards that "Samantha" was "Carol". I went to Boots that weekend and had an eyesight test and have worn glasses / contact lenses ever since. A true story. Only the names have been changed to protect the innocent. But I was guilty.

What advice would you have for young people just starting out in the world of banking / finance etc?

If you are setting out in the world of banking and finance, you have chosen an exceptional time to do so. Life is full of ups and downs. In economic terms, these turbulent times come about typically only every 10 years or so. But my experience is that you learn more about yourself and others in bad times rather than good times.

> " Always be prepared to ask -
> questions, favours, whatever;
> and always do your homework. "

James Mates

Journalism

Journalism

Journalism is the reporting, writing, editing, broadcasting or photographing of news to inform and/or educate the public. The field includes (to name but a few) newspaper and magazine editors, TV news presenters and radio broadcasters.

Journalists can report on various parts of news - sports, science, religion, international conflicts and politics. A good journalist must have a refined command of their native language and an ability to write and communicate effectively.

Some universities offer Journalism degrees but many journalists have degrees in other subjects, which develop and show their communication ability, such as a degree in English or a modern foreign language (e.g. German).

ANNE ATKINS

Novelist & Writer

Caption for photograph:
On an Afghan bus in the days when you could still get all the way to Nepal overland for a
fiver. Ok, I realise I may not look very glamorous (and I hadn't had a bath since Istanbul),
but the friend I was travelling with was offered a month's wages for a night with me. I
thought this was one up from the tray of Coca Cola he was offered the day before for my hand in marriage, until I
learnt that a bottle of coke cost a man's wages for a week or a woman's for two.

On the contrary, it's more a question wishing I knew now what I knew so effortlessly then.

If only I still knew, for instance, that although work is fun (and it was: I absolutely loved it)
sometimes simply having fun is more important.
I was doing four A levels: English, French, and History - Art, which filled all Monday and Friday afternoons. One
Friday, the musician Nic McGegan wanted to take me out for lunch and a drive. Not many of my friends had cars
and besides, Nic was endlessly fascinating. (One evening, while he was waiting to take me to a party, I heard him
tootling on the piano; not practising triplets against quavers as the rest of us might, but ninths against thirteenths
or something impossible. He used to read the New Testament for fun. In bed. In the original.) I guessed I could
probably get away with skipping triple art once, and did. But when Nic suggested the same the following Monday,
I knew I'd be pushing my luck. Most regretfully, I told my art teacher that my work load was too great, and dropped
the A level. Ah, if only I still had the confidence to abandon two years' work for a drive in the autumn sun...

I wish I knew as little about politics now as I did then - when I often read Shakespeare,
never a newspaper.
Our school staged a mock election before the General Election. Candidates put themselves
forward for Labour and Conservative, but none for the Liberals. When a teacher asked me to volunteer, in that way
that teachers have, I objected that I was planning to attend a chamber concert in the Fitzwilliam Museum (free in
those days) during the lunchtime hustings. She pointed out that I could leave after my speech, and still be on time
for the recital. This solved the problem of answering any challenging questions about Liberal policy, such as who
the leader was or what the party stood for. But the difficulty remained of delivering my impassioned plea for votes.
Happily, the evening before, Peter Bazlegette (then President of the Cambridge Union and now owner of Big Brother)
happened to call at our house. I shoved an envelope under his nose and he scribbled a speech on the back of it,
which I simply read out the next day. (To my embarrassment and regret, he only phrase I can remember now is that
my party would give feminists plenty of support out front.) As I jumped on my bike to get to the Fitzwilliam, the
applause for Peter's jokes was barely dying down. The following morning, a very worried Tory candidate for
Cambridge visited our head mistress to find out why such a Conservative stronghold had swung 90 percentage
points to the Liberals. Oh, if only I had still had Peter writing my scripts for me...

I wish I could be as unwittingly rude now, without causing offence.
One evening I was due to visit a friend in Queens' College. (I also wish I could mention such friends today without
sounding as if I were name-dropping, as I could before they had Done Things. All the most amusing people I knew
at school seem to have achieved far more than I have. This was Declan Donnellan, then merely a brilliant
undergraduate director, now founder of Cheek by Jowl.) I was rather late arriving, and found him looking beautifully
artistic lying on a chaise longue, reading a slim leather-bound novel by candlelight. "Oh Declan, I'm so sorry," I cried,
genuinely contrite, "you must have been posing for hours." If only I knew how to say such things today, and still have
my dinner bought for me...

True, when I was eighteen I didn't know how to make love, or give birth. I didn't know what it was to want another
person more than life itself, or to realise I would lay down my life for this scrap of humanity without a moment's
hesitation. I didn't know how to lie awake all night worrying about my children. I didn't know how to keep going year
after dark year, when there really is nothing left but the will which says hold on. I didn't know how to weep

spontaneously for a child the other side of the world, or be anxious about my own parents, or fret about what will happen to those dependent on me if I can't find work to replace what I've just lost. But it wouldn't be right to know such things at eighteen.

The trick is not to know, in youth, what you shouldn't know till half a lifetime later. The trick is still to remember, when you get there, what you knew so easily at eighteen...

MICHEAL BRUNSON

Journalist

In 1972, shortly after I arrived in Washington to begin my time as ITN's American correspondent, I put in a call to the Press Office of the United States Treasury with a query about the American economy. 'Thank you , Sir,' said a Press Officer, with that particular politeness with which Americans often seem to respond to a British accent, 'I'll have someone call you back.'

An hour or so later, an Assistant Secretary, the equivalent of a very senior Minister in Britain, was on the phone, asking for me. I was completely taken by surprise – a senior member of the American administration, taking the time to call little me, a newly arrived and very green young British journalist, in order to give me a personal briefing. It gave my confidence an enormous boost at the start of an important stage in my career.

But it did more. It underlined for me the fact that, at heart, people invested with power and authority and influence are, nonetheless, just ordinary human beings like you and me. It was, if you like, living proof of the old saying 'Surely a cat can look at a king!'. Indeed the cat can, and very often should. Furthermore, the cat should not just look, but approach the king and try and ask whatever he wants to ask, even if the king doesn't deign to reply, or even appear to notice that the cat is there.

I wish I had realised that when I was 18. I wish I had gained that degree of self-confidence much earlier in my career, instead of saying to myself far too often 'Oh, I'm sure he or she won't want to talk to me' or 'What if he or she is annoyed by my request, or slams the phone down on me?' Part of that was the fear of rejection, or the risk of making myself appear cheeky or stupid, but during my time in America, I began to develop a thicker skin, and I wish I'd acquired that by the time I was 18, too.

10 years or so later, I learnt something else which I wish I'd realised much earlier. An incident at the end of a summit meeting in the German capital at the time, Bonn, reminded me that too much self-confidence, going too far in the other direction, is just as much of a handicap as having too little. During a press conference being held by the German Chancellor of the day, Helmut Schmidt, and the then British Prime Minister, Margaret Thatcher, I got up in front of a hundred or so journalists, and asked what I thought was a very clever question. It was, however, all too apparent from the gradual murmuring around the room, even as I was speaking, that I was making a complete fool of myself. In case I thought otherwise, Mrs Thatcher leaned towards her Press Secretary, Bernard Ingham, and in the biggest stage whisper you can imagine, and clearly audible to plenty of other people, simply said 'What a very stupid question!'

During my time at Bedford, I learnt both Latin and Greek, and was a member of a tiny number of pupils in what was then known as the 'Classical Sixth'. It was hard and difficult work, and I'm pretty certain that I should have been a historian, but that education in the classics at least introduced me to an old and valuable Greek motto. Inscribed above the entrance to the cave where the legendary Delphic Oracle could be consulted was written, according to the legend, the words 'Know Thyself'. It's very wise advice. 'Know thyself ' - strengths and weaknesses, when to push ahead and when to hold back. Had I paid more attention to that famous saying when I was younger, I think I would have developed a better balance between too little and too much self-confidence rather earlier in my life.

But, hey! Life's about making plenty of mistakes and learning from them, and I was especially fortunate. It certainly wasn't all heavy going – and during 40 years of front-line journalism, I enjoyed, not just a stimulating and satisfying career, but an awful lot of fun as well.

JAMES MATES

Senior Correspondent of ITV News

I'm the senior correspondent of ITV News, a foreign correspondent basically, who's been working the same coal-face of international news for more than 25 years now. There have been many interesting times, and inevitably some less-interesting ones, but never dull times. However, much waiting around for things to happen (and every journalist has done a lot of that) you never lose the excitement of what might happen, of what your competition might be up to, of how you are going to make some pretty average events that day interesting enough to be worth a slot on the evening news bulletin.

If you love going places, meeting people, seeing world events happen in front of you, never doing the same thing two days in a row, (and I do) there is no better way to earn a living.

I've been doing it since I was 21, but lets go a little further back: if there is one thing I wish someone could have convinced me of when I was just 18 it is this: that when you ask someone for something, they usually say 'yes'. If they don't, when you ask them a second time, they'll usually change their mind. Teachers, doctors, officials, parents, contacts, politicians, girls. Just ask nicely, be prepared to be a bit persistent, and as long as the request isn't totally unreasonable, a positive response is almost always there for the having in the end. I'm no psychologist, but it seems to me that there is something in the human condition that leads us to want to be agreeable, to be helpful, to say yes when we can. Not everyone, of course, but the thing that is hard to remember when nervously starting out in the world of work is that when you do come up against a solid and immovable 'no', nothing has been lost expect, perhaps, a little bit of pride. And, frankly, you can't afford to have too much of that anyway.

I had an unusual start in journalism in that I started in national news, skipping the usual apprentice period in local or regional newsrooms before heading for London. This, obviously, had its advantages, but it wasn't an unmixed blessing; a lot was expected very quickly by people who were themselves very good at their jobs. Learning on the job from the best in the business is both a privilege and a challenge. They are not always the best, or the most patient, teachers. In fact many don't appear to want you anywhere near them. But my experience was that they were all susceptible to flattery. There is no one who doesn't enjoy being looked up to, being made to feel that they are the master of their chosen profession, an oracle to whom others are coming in search of wisdom. And when you make them feel like that, they suddenly become very willing to share their wisdom, to let you in on the secrets, the techniques, the hard-learned tricks of the trade that have made them stand out above their competition. It's that thing again of being willing to ask.

I was lucky enough to work for many months during the great miners strike of 1984-5 with a senior and respected correspondent who was always happy to share anything he knew. Of course I had to do my job, and do it properly and well. No one is going to help a colleague they think to be incompetent or lazy. But when, in quiet moments, I would praise his skill or flair in the coverage of some event or another, and ask interestedly why he had chosen to do or say something in a particular way (so much better than the competition had managed), the accumulated knowledge of years on the road would flow forth. And in the course of it I learned almost everything I know about how to do my job.

The happy result was that when an opportunity came my way I was, at least in part, ready to seize it. The first time I had a chance to do anything on national television came on a bitterly cold Saturday afternoon at a coal mine near Barnsley where Arthur Scargill, the fire-brand leader of the National Union of Mineworkers was due to visit a picket line. Not much was expected from it, so I was sent alone and unsupervised. What happened was that he did have something rather important to say, and in the media scrum I became separated from my cameraman. Rather than standing alongside each other, I was facing Scargill while the camera was behind him. What followed was an interview in which one could only see the back of the subject's head, while the only thing viewers saw on the lead story of the news that night was me asking questions. Not ideal, but for a young would-be reporter certainly an opportunity to get noticed. I was, thank goodness, prepared.

In terms of rules to live by those are my two principle guides. Always be prepared to ask - questions, favours, whatever; and always do your homework. It is not rocket science, it's true, but I certainly wish I'd known them sooner.

And there is a third, perhaps more a mantra than a principle, but it's one I have to remind myself of constantly. 'See pressure as an opportunity'. When things are straightforward, no one is going to be particularly impressed that you have done a good job. Certainly no one will have any reason to remember it. But get into a situation in which you are really up against it, in which you could easily fail and make a fool of yourself, and people are going to be pleasantly surprised if you even survive, let alone thrive. Suddenly you have an opportunity. And when I'm nervous, and I wonder if I'm going to hold things together, and I can't think clearly because my mind is filled with panicked images of how horrible this could become, I try to say to myself 'pressure is an opportunity. Pull this one off and you're going to look really impressive. Right here and now is a rare chance to stand-out, so be happy'.

Apart from that, you're on your own!

ROBERT PESTON

BBC Business Editor

I am the BBC's Business Editor, which means that I spend a crazy amount of time broadcasting (on TV and radio) and writing (my blog at bbc.co.uk/robertpeston) about domestic and global business issues. My overwhelming aim is to present stories so that all our audience, and not just specialists, feel that business and economics really matters to them. For the past 25 years, I have been a journalist (for the FT, Independent and Sunday Telegraph, among others). In that time, I have been a Financial Editor, a Political Editor, a columnist and a head of an investigations unit (which I set up).

The main contributors to any success I have achieved are tenacity, attention to detail, a hunger to find things out, an obsession with factual accuracy, a horror of compromising my imartiality, a refusal to cut corners, and sheer love of the job.

For most of my career, I have concentrated on trying to get scoops. In a way the most important breakthroughs have been sticking to my guns when criticised for disclosing information that some would have preferred kept quiet. What I wish I had known when starting out in my career is that some older people will give bad advice - sometimes because they are not as wise as they think they may be and sometimes because they feel threatened by young people. But it really is important to listen to those with experience and authority, even if ultimately you choose not to do what they suggest.

My counsel to young people is don't rush into a career, try a few things out, evaluate your strengths and weaknesses, assess what gives you satisfaction and don't be demoralised by setbacks. Once you're clear about what you want to do, give it your best shot and stick at it. If you give up at the first obstacle, you may never forgive yourself.

Blog: http://bbc.co.uk/robertpeston.

The importance of empathy should
never be underestimated either –
good lawyers always listen to their clients.

David Dickinson

Law

Law

Law is a system of rules to govern the conduct of a community, society or nation. The subject can be further broken down into many components parts: Criminal law, contract law, tax law, human rights law, immigration law and family law, to name but a few!

The word "lawyer" refers to any one who practices law, solicitors and barristers are the well-known jobs within law but others exist as well, such as clerks, paralegals and legal executives.

If you think you have strong argumentative, analytical and communication skills a career in law could be for you. Although many solicitors and barristers have studied law at university, it is a common misconception that this is the only way to get into law. In fact many people study a different subject at degree level and then do a one (or two) year course to become lawyers. A number of years practical experience in a firm/chambers is also required.

MARK DAWKINS

Lawyer

When I was a sixth form and university student, I did not really know what I wanted to do and, for that reason, decided to keep my options open. This led me to study law, because I thought that it would lead to a broad range of job opportunities. Before I went to university, I had no experience of law at all and none of my family had ever been members of the legal profession. So, it was uncharted territory for me.

Throughout my time at University, I stuck to the strategy of keeping my options open, thinking that I might want to go into banking or finance, or do something else "in business". However, as I came to the end of my three year degree course, I decided that I ought to do something practical about my career and that, as I had spent three years of my life studying law, I ought to round it off by going to law school. In those days, the mandatory one year professional qualification at law college had a bad reputation amongst university law students: there was little scope for deep thinking on legal issues, but enormous amounts of data to be learned by rote.

I was therefore surprised to find that, once I had started my course at law college, I actually enjoyed it. What I enjoyed was the fact that at law college students learned about things that made law relevant to the real world. I can recall attending a lecture when we were all taught about how to interview a distressed client, seeking protection from a violent spouse. As it turned out, this particular lecture had no direct relevance at all to my subsequent career, but it brought home to me, for the first time, that the practice of law is fundamentally about the rights and responsibilities of people; and this firmly captured my interest.

This interest in people has stayed with me throughout my career at Simmons & Simmons. I qualified as a commercial litigation solicitor and, although almost all of my work has been for major companies and banks, within those organisations you are always dealing with individuals, whether as clients, witnesses, expert advisers and so on.

One of my earliest memories at Simmons & Simmons was the thrill that I got from discovering that important people would not only listen to what I said (even as a trainee lawyer), but would follow my advice and, remarkably, be happy to pay the firm for it! In many ways, I think this is still what defines my enjoyment of the profession today, and I expect it is true about people in other professions as well: it is a great thing to be highly trained in a particular expertise and then to use that expertise to help others to solve problems or otherwise achieve the outcomes that they are looking for.

People often ask me about the stresses of the legal profession. It is true that we work hard, but then so do many other people in different careers. In any event, working hard is not in my view a cause of stress. Work-related stress is very often caused by worrying about things that you have not done, or been unable to do. I find that the best answer to this is to have a supportive, working environment and a culture where you can share your problems with colleagues, and know that they will try to help you. I have been fortunate always to have worked in such an environment and that is one of the main reasons that I have spent all my working life at Simmons & Simmons.

DAVID DICKINSON

Solicitor, Senior Partner at Simmons & Simmons

What was your first ever job?
My first job after leaving school and before starting my articles (legal training contract) was selling Scalextrics (which worked) and diesel model aircraft (which often didn't) at a well known store. I was paid £11 a week.

How did you make your first steps to success (in particular becoming senior partner at Simmons & Simmons), and what do you consider to be the key to your success?
I would say the key to success in law, and any chosen profession, is hard work and having an open mind when opportunities arise. I started my career at age 18 with a five year training contract. (At that time you didn't need to have a degree to qualify as a lawyer.) Therefore I was put before my first client at a very young age. Looking back I can understand why clients did not take me seriously at that age but it gave me (at least) a very interesting experience. During my training period I did everything from divorce to corporate transactions and some fairly esoteric tax advice, consequently I had to deal with a very broad range of people. I found that variation an indispensable experience.

After I qualified and having spent a few years with my first firm I moved on to a major City firm, which gave me first class experience in international finance transactions. I then worked for United Bank of Switzerland (Securities) Ltd for a few years which gave me a significant understanding of the workings of financial institutions and the experience of being a client rather than a lawyer. I joined Simmons &Simmons 20 years ago to set up the firm's capital markets practice.

What is the most exciting deal you have worked on and why?
In 1980 I was asked by a Kuwaiti institution to act for them on an investment they were making into a Japanese electronics company. I really enjoyed working with the individual from the client, who was a Kuwaiti. The transaction was the first of its type and was aimed at encouraging increased Middle East investment of "petro dollars" into the Japanese market. It was my first experience with Japan and was the first time I led on such an innovative transaction. Ever since I have retained an interest in Japan and its culture.

What do you wish you had known when you were younger?
I wasn't a great success at school. I'm not quite sure why, but I'm sure that one problem was I didn't put enough into it. In those days getting back to where you should be if you didn't follow the routine path was difficult (but not as difficult as it is now).

Do you have a personal mantra?
You can achieve whatever you like but the chances are it will take you longer and will be more difficult than you think. So clear goals and tenacity are important.

What is the best thing about your job?
I travel a good deal and meet a lot of people - people who work in my firm (who are an extremely talented, intelligent and motivated people) and also meeting the firm's clients, all of which I enjoy very much.
What advice would you have for young people just starting out in the world of law?
Remain open minded about the area of law in which you want to practise. Take every opportunity to gather broad and wide experience.

How do you deal with the stresses of work?
Work is a great challenge and one which I enjoy greatly but it is important to maintain broad interest outside of the office. However my main support has been my family.

In your opinion, what qualities are demanded of an aspiring solicitor?
Integrity, hard work and a sharp mind. The importance of empathy should never be underestimated either – good lawyers always listen to their clients.

MIKE EDWARDS

Lawyer

What attracted you to a profession in law?
The challenge of a demanding discipline which has a significant commercial component with a varied workload.

How did you make your first steps to success and what do you consider to be the key to your success?
I was lucky to obtain training with a successful city centre law firm in Manchester and worked with very good lawyers who were not afraid to share their knowledge and experience and had a keen interest in developing young lawyers.

I try to learn from each transaction, never believe you have got it all right and know everything there is to know.

What have been your most valuable career-defining experiences?
That you can always learn from other people, but you have to have an open enquiring mind and be prepared to listen, to discuss views and concerns.

What do you wish you had known when you were younger?
How precious time is and the need to make the most of every opportunity.

Are there any funny/comic moments that you can remember from your career?
There are lots of comic and memorable moments but for fear of lawsuits and the laws of libel I had better keep them to myself!

What advice would you have for young people just starting out in the world of law?
It is a very competitive, challenging environment that is very well worth embracing for talented and committed students. It provides a lot of rewarding personal experiences, more than just financial, to people of ability, enthusiasm, commitment and flexibility.

Is there anything else you would like to add?
Not really, but I will add that keeping an enquiring mind and open attitude have served me well.

> ## Ignore all the politics. Concentrate on doing a good job and you will be recognised.

Dr Graham Wylie

Medicine

Medicine

One of the most demanding professions, medicine remains a favourite among students as their first choice career. The field covers a huge range of disciplines and offers opportunities to specialise in many areas such as dermatology or neurology. As it is so competitive, university admissions tutors will expect higher qualifications in chemistry, biology and even maths when hiring. Previous work experience in hospitals or other medical practices is usually essential in securing a place at university.

With the largest employer in the UK, the NHS, on the lookout for people in this field, medical students find it fairly easy to find work. However it is not an easy career. You will need to be dedicated and be able to absorb huge amounts of information in short periods of time as well as having good communication skills. Working hours can be long and the medical training takes a long time.

Doctors must be registered with the General Medical Council (GMC) to practice medicine in the UK and other careers within medicine also have similar requirements.

DR. CHARLOTTE FOWLER

Consultant Radiologist

When I was 18 I had no idea what I wanted to do. I remember very clearly sitting in the school library with a pencil hovering over my university application form and praying that wherever it dropped it might at least lead to something interesting. It certainly landed on something strange and wonderful, a course in Agriculture and Forestry at Oxford University where I spent many happy hours tromping around forests and farms (which have since formed the backdrop to various Morse episodes) learning about the application of biology to the real world.

When my time at college was drawing to an end, I still had no sense of direction and (now feeling rather panicky), I applied for a graduate management trainee post in a large food firm, Rank Hovis McDougall. Here I worked in three disciplines, computing, human resources and marketing, ending up working on the marketing of McDougalls flour! I worked with wonderful people, learnt a great deal about business and enjoyed myself very much, but still had an uneasy feeling that this was not quite the right environment for me.

Then out of the blue came the inspiration and desire to train to become a doctor and 5 years at medical school and 10 years of post graduate training later, I am now a consultant radiologist, working with teams of other doctors, nurses and radiographers to diagnose patient's diseases using the range of imaging techniques such as ultrasound, CT, MRI and x-rays. It is a great investigative 'medical Sherlock Holmes' job, and I especially enjoy the research I do as I feel my contribution may influence the wellbeing, not only to the patients I come into direct contact with, but also possibly a wider population in the future.

People ask me if I would have preferred to have done medicine at the conventional age of 18 rather than coming to it in my mid 20s, but I really feel that I used the skills I learnt during my science degree at Oxford and my time in business every day and that they have probably made me into a better doctor than I would have been had I gone straight into medicine from school. As an example of this, medical statistics are based on agricultural statistics, so I still apply the knowledge and skills I gained from my first degree when analysing research results, and my time in business gave me the understanding of how to put together a successful business plan for medical and research projects which may otherwise not have succeeded.

What I wish I had known at 18 is that as long as you enjoy what you do and work really hard you really don't have to worry about finding the right track; doors will open to the right path, given an open mind, ambition to achieve, a touch of luck and the courage to respond to life's opportunities. Oh, and find senior people along the way whose opinions you trust, ask their advice and take it!

Enjoy!

DR. JINDA ROJANAMATIN

Head of Dermatosurgery & Laser Department,
Institute of Dermatology, Bangkok, Thailand

Dr Rojanamatin is the head of dermatosurgery and laser department at the Institute of Dermatology in Bangkok, Thailand, and a noted lecture for major laser companies. He gained a diploma in Dermatology from the Thai Board and now has 20 years of experience in corrective, surgical and cosmetic dermatology under his belt. His experience is vast having obtained a certificate in cosmetic dermatology in Miami, where he studied the uses of Botox and derma fillers, and received a fellowship in laser surgery from Tokyo.

What qualifications do you need to have a career in medicine?

Firstly you have to have graduated as a doctor of medicine, this takes 6 years. Following this, to become a dermatologist, there is a requirement of 1 year of dermatology training, followed by 3 years residency in an accredited dermatology residency program. The first year's residency is to qualify you as a doctor, and the next three help you to train for this specialised field.

What skills or qualities are required to become a dermatologist?

In my opinion, there are two pre-requisites to be a successful dermatologist:

- To be willing to acquire new knowledge. As a dermatologist you must be willing to acquire the know-how to improve your treatment techniques with the most efficient tools and equipments as they are developed.
- To be able to cope with both responsibility and professional integrity. As a dermatologist, I have to diagnose and provide a range of treatment including surgery, phototherapy, dermabrasions (removing superficial layers of skin), Botox injections and laser therapy treatment. Hence, it is crucial to apply the appropriate treatment and consider the patient safety as first priority, otherwise, there may be side-effects that are difficult to correct and cure.

Do you have a personal mantra?

My mantra is "To make patients happy with utmost care, highest integrity, and to be warm, pleasant and competent."

What attracted you to becoming a dermatologist and what would you say will attract young people to follow such a career?

If you are considering a career in medicine but are unsure about which field to specialise in, one place you may want to look is the field of dermatology. Along with traditional dermatologists who deal with skin diseases, the growth in cosmetic surgery is fuelling a need for more specialised doctors. This demand is leading to higher wages and a promising career development. Technology offers treatments today that only a few years ago would have been scoffed at and called impossible. Who would have believed radio waves would tighten skin, not just on a surface level but on a structural level! Dermatologists have been given the unique opportunity to make genuine differences in people's self-confidence and appearance. As a physician, nothing is more gratifying than knowing your skills and training have made a patient "better" -whether that "better" by adding confidence to go about everyday life knowing that aging or wrinkled skin is no longer a worry.

DAVID BRETT WILLIAMS

Optometric Director, Specsavers Opticians

Profession/short job description:
Optometrist (Optometric Director Specsavers opticians)

How did you make your first steps to success, and what do you consider to be the key to your success?
I changed university degrees even though I had 'lost' four years of studying in doing so. I moved into a profession with greater opportunities.

What have been you most valuable career-defining experiences?
Working in nasty jobs during the summers while at university. I swore that I would not be doing this in later years. However, it motivated me to study harder and get my degrees.

What do you wish you had known when you were younger?
The growth potential of different professions. For example in 2006, there were 7500 accountants in the UK. They made an average £48,000 pounds. The growth potential in that field is 10% per annum with salaries increasing at 14% p.a. Then I could make a balanced decision whether or not I wanted to enter that profession.

What advice would you have for young people just starting out in the world of business?
Love you're product enough to be passionate about it, but not too much that it blinds your decision making process. Sometimes we love our product too much, that we don't see, that customers don't want or need it.

DR. GRAHAM WYLIE

CEO of The Medical Research Network

Profession/short job description:
CEO of The Medical Research Network. I own and run a small company that supports the running of clinical trials in the UK.

How did you make your first steps to success, and what do you consider to be the key to your success?
I moved out of medical practice (I am a physician) and joined the pharmaceutical industry.
What has enabled me to be successful is a willingness to learn about what I do, explore areas outside my immediate job that allow me to understand the broader picture and to strive to improve the way I and others work.

What have been your most valuable career-defining experiences?
Working abroad in corporate HQ in New York.
Leaving my first company after 10 years to join a company that would expose me to research on a commercial footing. Buying my division from the company I worked for to set up on my own.

What do you wish you had known when you were younger?
What the broader opportunities are in the world. Of course get a good job and good training in your chosen field, but more significant rewards are available for those who branch out and ensure they get all the experiences they need to run their own business.

What advice would you have for young people just starting out in the world of business?
Never resent working hard. Take on new challenges. Always try to learn. Have an idea of where you want to go but don't over plan your career – take opportunities as they present themselves.

Is there anything else that you would like to add?
Ignore all the politics. Concentrate on doing a good job and you will be recognised. Treat each job as a way of making yourself more employable and move on when you stop learning from your job. Always remember, it's what you actually deliver that counts. Be a 'donor' rather than a 'taker'

" Try to be kind to people – unless they're trying to kill you!! "

Wing Commander Roy Gamblin AFC

Military

Military

Being a member of the armed forces, you will have the important role of protecting your country and aiding people in times of desperate need. Travelling around the country and the world could be one of the benefits of being in the military, as it will offer a chance to broaden your mind and widen your perspective of the world.

In contrast, you may have to bear great responsibilities, the intense physical and mental hardship and the obvious fact that in battle you are risking your own life and potentially changing others'.

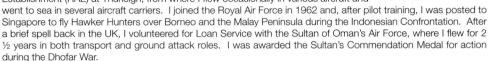

WING COMMANDER ROY GAMBLIN AFC

Aviator

Profession/short job description:

I caught the flying bug early in my first job as a Scientific Assistant at the Royal Aircraft Establishment (RAE) at Thurleigh, from where I flew occasionally in various aircraft and went to sea in several aircraft carriers. I joined the Royal Air Force in 1962 and, after pilot training, I was posted to Singapore to fly Hawker Hunters over Borneo and the Malay Peninsula during the Indonesian Confrontation. After a brief spell back in the UK, I volunteered for Loan Service with the Sultan of Oman's Air Force, where I flew for 2 ½ years in both transport and ground attack roles. I was awarded the Sultan's Commendation Medal for action during the Dhofar War.

In 1971, after training at the RAF Central Flying School, I became a flying instructor and Flight Commander for 3 years at the RAF's Advanced Flying Training School at RAF Valley on Anglesey, where I met and married my wife, June. We moved to Norway when I was posted as the RAF exchange pilot for 2 years on a Royal Norwegian Air Force fighter squadron. Promotion to Squadron Leader led me back to Valley to command the Standards Squadron during the introduction to the RAF of the new Hawk jet trainer. For my work there in Hunter, Gnat, and Hawk aircraft, I was awarded an Air Force Cross in 1979. After attending the RAF Advanced Staff Course at Bracknell, and a short tour as a planner at HQ Strike Command, I was promoted to Wing Commander and served my last RAF post in command of the Harrier Operations Wing at RAF Wittering from 1982-84.

I did my 'commercial apprenticeship' on the ground for 4 years, mainly as the Sales and Marketing Director for a manufacturer of flying and security equipment in Wheathampstead. The work involved much travel in opening new markets from Australia to the United States. I kept my hand in as a pilot at weekends with the RAF Volunteer Reserve. The call back to aviation was strong and I returned to full-time flying for over 11 years with the Civil Aircraft Division of British Aerospace. There, I qualified as an airline training captain, examiner, demonstration pilot, test pilot and project manager and spent much time with many customer airlines worldwide including in the USA, the Caribbean, Europe, Turkey, China, Bangladesh, Indonesia and New Zealand. For my work over a 3-year period in setting up a major European operation using Avro RJ airliners from Brussels (to where I commuted weekly from NW Wales!) I received a BAe Chairman's Award for Innovation.

In 2000, I was grounded with a cardiac condition, now fixed but leaving me unable to fly as a pilot; and so I retired to my home by the coast in the Snowdonia National Park. I write articles for an aviation enthusiasts' group and have spent several years building a superb replica of a Jaguar XK 120. I completed a BSc with the Open University in 1996. I am a keen and frequent hill-walker. I speak a little Welsh and am still fairly fluent in Norwegian. I have been a member of the OB Club since leaving School in 1960 and was elected President in September 2007.

How did you make your first steps to success, and what do you consider to be the key to your success?

The first step was an interview with the Bedford School Careers Master. That led to my first job, as a scientific assistant in the Naval Air Department at RAE Thurleigh. The next two crucial steps were:
- Having the cheek, at age 17, to ask the RAF if I could join them to train as a pilot when, following my attendance at the Aircrew Selection Centre at RAF Biggin Hill, they had only seen fit to offer me training as an Air Electronics Officer – they accepted my plea.
- Volunteering, at age 23, for loan service with the Sultan of Oman's Air Force. I did most of my growing up there and, unknowingly at the time, the responsibilities that were given to me laid firm foundations for later career advancement.

Apart from the excellent all-round education provided to me by Bedford School, the key to success was perhaps my desire to enjoy myself in my work. However, I was yet to learn that it was often necessary to put as much energy into the less enjoyable tasks, as the more enjoyable ones, since that usually served the overall aim of achieving enjoyment!! Bedford had tried to instil that within me, of course, but in that respect I was to be a slow learner!!

What have been your most valuable career-defining experiences?

There have been so many, but I'll try to list the most important ones in chronological order:

- Flying as an observer in aircraft at Thurleigh and spending several weeks at sea in aircraft carriers supporting RAE flight trials – sparked a lifelong interest in aviation.
- Training to be an RAF pilot – provided the best possible training for an aviator.
- Serving as an operational fighter/ground attack pilot for several years in each of temperate, tropical, desert and arctic environments – gave a very wide view of the World from many aspects, both in flight and on the ground.
- Becoming a qualified flying instructor and teaching at the RAF's Advanced Flying Training School for 6 years, including as an examiner and, for the final 3 years, Head of Training Standards for all instructors and students. Teaching and helping others to meet high standards provided the means to identify how I could best improve my own skills and knowledge.
- Having a key role in introducing the new Hawk jet trainer into RAF service – provided excellent experience for carving out leading management roles in large and complex projects.
- Completing the one-year RAF Advanced Staff Course – gave a very much wider window on life, work and the World than the view from the cockpit or through a military aviator's eyes.
- Spending 6 months as an aviation consultant then three years as a Sales and Marketing Director in varied international markets - provided my "Commercial Apprenticeship".
- Working worldwide for British Aerospace as an airline training captain, licensed examiner (for the civil aviation authorities of many countries), test pilot, demonstration pilot and project manager – gave me the peak of fulfilment as an aviator and senior manager.
- Managing (over 3 years and jointly with my Belgian counterpart) the operational aspects of introducing 32 new jet airliners into European service with the Belgian National Airline, Sabena. The project included recruiting over 50 contract pilots at the outset and then training over 300 pilots of 10 different nationalities – it probably wore me out prematurely!!!!

What do you wish you had known when you were younger?

- That "Selection and maintenance of the aim" - the First Principle of War as taught in the British Armed Services - is a useful principle in almost everything one does in life.
- That a job worth doing is worth doing well.
- The importance of consensus rather than confrontation.
- The need to smile as much as possible!
- That one should always try to maintain an escape route from very difficult or very dangerous situations.
- That one should never trust "the local expert" without question. Trust your own instincts too.
- That it's vital to anticipate problems before they arise and plan solutions to them, rather than wait for them to pop up unexpectedly.
- The importance of maintaining morale in your subordinates and praising them for their efforts, as well as their results.

Do you have a personal Mantra?

Yes. Never be afraid to try something that interests you even if you might think it's beyond your capabilities.

Are there any funny / comic moments that you can remember from your career?

Many – but they all take too long too explain or they rely too much on "in" knowledge!!

What advice would you have for young people just starting out in the world?

Choose a career primarily for its enjoyment and satisfaction and never primarily for the money.

Is there anything else that you would like to add?

Try to be kind to people – unless they're trying to kill you!!

LIEUTENANT COLONEL SIMON WILKINSON TD, DL, FNAEA

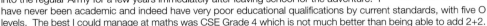

When I was at Cedars Comprehensive School in Leighton Buzzard in the 1970's I did not know what I wanted to do when I left school. My father had a very enjoyable two years as the National Service Officer in the 1950's and my strongest thoughts were to go into the regular Army for a few years immediately after leaving school for the adventure. I have never been academic and indeed have very poor educational qualifications by current standards, with five O levels. The best I could manage at maths was CSE Grade 4 which is not much better than being able to add 2+2.

In terms of my success I think the biggest advantage I have had is being able to identify people to whom I could relate and for whom I had a certain amount of respect and probably most importantly these were also people that were not patronising but talked to me at my level. In particular I remember my Economics teacher at Cedars School who was very helpful and talked a lot of common sense. I left school at 17 and went to Aylesbury College to do an OND in Business Studies. This course was very relevant for going into business and we were treated like adults. I found this much more motivational. It was at this time that I was advised to join the Territorial Army and did so at the age of 17½. Some 28 years later and now aged 45 I have a huge amount to thank the TA for, regarding the experiences it has given me. At 18 when I left school I joined the family business of John Wilkinson Estate Agents and in a very short space of time I was given relatively large amounts of responsibility and with sensible guidance from the various managers over a period of years learnt a huge amount from these inspirational and motivational people in the sales environment.

This combined with the training I had through the TA and ultimately being commissioned at Sandhurst in 1987 meant that I gained significant amounts of confidence and the ability to communicate effectively with people and most importantly understand what motivated and drove people. I think that being able to motivate and inspire people to achieve their best is a wonderful thing and I cherish it dearly.

As my business has grown and developed I have taken on added responsibility and this has also been the same in the TA. In 2003 I was "called up" and went to Iraq for a six month tour on operations across Iraq. This was a life changing experience and exposed me to Heads of State and Ministers from over thirty countries. I had never expected in my younger days to have been advising Ministers and Prime Ministers on policy matters! In 1996 I attended a "Common Purpose" programme in Milton Keynes which introduced people from the public, private and voluntary sector to issues that related to the society and community in the area. This course was 12 months in duration and was an extremely valuable learning opportunity and introduced me to people that under normal circumstances I would not have met. This has enabled me to network with these contacts for everyone's benefit.

What do I wish I had known when I was younger?

I think with hindsight it would have been that there are a lot of jobs that are safer and more secure than running an estate agency. I think also that common sense is often much more valuable than academic brilliance and the ability to communicate effectively with people is a hugely important life skill. If I had a personal mantra it would be that if you are honest and fair with people they will be honest and fair with you – at least most of the time. Also that making mistakes is part of the learning process but that making the same mistake twice is your own fault. There are lots of funny things that have happened to me in my career, for example showing a couple of prospective buyers around what was thought to be an empty house only to find the lady of the house in the bath. For young people starting out in the world my advice would be to travel to second and third world countries only, for several months to see and appreciate the wider world within which we live, to always be prepared to take risks, to know in your own heart whether you are honest - to yourself and to others.

Finally I believe I have already packed a huge amount into 45 years of my life and have already done many things that a lot of other people would not have achieved in several lives. Always believe in yourself but never be afraid to place trust in others, it will surprise you!

Stick with it.
Remember Charles Darwin spent years
and years studying and accumulating
information, before he changed the
world for ever.

Adam Hart-Davis

Miscellaneous

Miscellaneous

We have been very lucky to receive advice from a wide range of professions. However, we have been unable to create individual categories for each job type. Instead we have collated these people into one varied chapter, whose line of work does not fit in with the other categories. You will still find them useful as they have plenty of advice to offer from the various professions.

In this final chapter, we have advice from an actress, artist, art valuer, author, civil engineer, top public relations specialist, a well known inventor, health and fitness expert, hairstylist professor, TV personality and many more... To name just a few of the great diverse range of people and professions we have in this chapter.

TREVOR BAYLISS

INVENTOR

My Brilliant Career

My profession?– I call myself an inventor. Why not? You can call yourself an artist, scientist, or engineer. But remember we are all inventors. I believe there is an idea in all of us. I also believe that chance favours the prepared mind. I came to where I am now by a very circuitous route.

I grew up in London during the War. I lived in a part of London that was hit by constant bombing from enemy aircraft. As a result, electricity wasn't always available and many household chores were done manually – washing was done by hand and hung in the garden, candles often replaced light bulbs, Mum's iron rested on the stove, and the allotment garden provided much or our food. Having grown up like this I appreciate more than most the benefits of modern technology, but it was also the beginning of my interest in human powered machines which lead to my invention, the Clockwork Radio.

The first steps to success for me were taken when I was given a Meccano set as a child. I could not do maths but learned to build the most fantastic constructions using my imagination.

I had failed my 11+ exam, but by the time I was 19 I had studied mechanical and structural engineering at technical colleges – I did this whilst working in a soil mechanics lab. It was day part time release programme.

I learned to swim when I was eight years old, and guess what? By the time I was 15 I was swimming for Great Britain. Interest in sport lead to my working as a physical training instructor while in the army when I was doing my National Service . This lead to stunt work and work as professional swimmer.

One of the most exciting adventures in my life was when I performed as an underwater escape artiste at a circus at the Deutschland halle in Berlin. I was dressed as Ramses II and had to escape from a sarcophagus nailed shut and submerged in a tank of water. Working with stunt people and circus performers made me realise that many of my friends had injuries acquired from the hazards of their profession had a lot in common with disabled people. They were kinfolk. Disability is only a banana skin away.

This led me to create over 300 products for those who are disabled. They were called Orange Aids. Years later, listening to a programme on AIDS in Africa, I was inspired to invent the Clockwork Radio.

There is an expression: Chance favours the prepared mind. I believe there is an invention in all of us. If you can solve a problem, you are well on your way to becoming an inventor. The use of the word 'great' with invention can only be determined by the user of that invention.

If you are in a bad way health wise, a chair lift might be the best invention of all time. Remember inventions must be judged both socially and commercially. The best inventions of all times meet both demands.

Our economy was grown on the back of great British inventions. I am trying to raise the profile of inventors in this country. They are thought of as oily rags, or oddballs with Viennese accents and crooked glasses. But the contribution their work and ingenuity has made to our lives is incalculable.

Things I wished I had known when I was young ? I wish I had understood intellectual property when I began to invent products. I learned about it the hard way. What is this? A Patent is a license granted to an inventor which gives him the legal right to his idea and protection from having his idea used by someone else. Nobody pays you for a good idea but will pay you for a piece of paper which says you own that idea – a patent, copyright, design registration or trademark. Having a patent protects your idea from being stolen by others.

Also I didn't understand disclosure – if you go down to the pub and tell everyone your idea – you have given your idea away and cannot now theoretically be protected.

The man who inspired me most was the 21 year old Frank Whittle who invented the jet engine – had government listened to him WWII would have been WW1 ½ !! As soon as his patent was published, the Germans recognised immediately its value and importance, and had jet planes flying before us.

My advice is always follow your heart. If you really enjoy water skiing- do it, you never know where it might lead you – It is so important to enjoy your life.

If you have a good idea do something about it – do not put yourself in a position where because you have done nothing about it that you wake up 20 years later and see it in a shop window etc.

MICHAEL ROLAND BLACK

Chartered Civil Engineer

I am a Chartered Civil Engineer who has worked on major international civil engineering projects throughout my chosen career since leaving Bedford School, i.e. 50 years ago!I initially worked solely in the UK, working on the construction of highway projects such as the Warwick and Oxford By-Passes. In 1977, a major UK recession saw a massive downturn in UK Civil Engineering which forced me to seek work elsewhere, i.e. overseas. I have subsequently had the privilege of working on the construction of Mass Transit Systems (i.e. Metros) in Hong Kong, Singapore, Bangkok - Thailand, New Delhi – India and now in Dubai, UAE. My role has been that of a Project Manager on behalf of International Contractors (mainly Japanese) responsible for completing Projects "on time and within budget". At the tender age of 67 years old, I am now working on the Dubai Metro, a Project comprising some 32,000 workers with a targeted dedicated opening date of 9 September 2009 (i.e. 9/9/9) which will be achieved.

When I left school, I had no idea what I wanted to do! I did, however, have several thoughts as to what I didn't want to do which were:

- Work in an office.
- Stay in the same place.
- Wear a suit to work!

By process of elimination, the world of Civil Engineering had a distinct appeal. This was at the same time when the MI Motorway was under construction and the thought of working out of doors and travelling (even if it was only to the adjacent County), gave me the freedom for which I was searching.

That was how it all started – the next County became the whole world and offices were replaced with major construction sites and working with multi-national personnel.

I have no regrets as to my chosen career and even now, get a thrill seeing a completed Project in use by the general public.

It must be remembered, that in the type of work I do, I have always been an employee as opposed to an employer. Success (in the world of Civil Engineering and employed by International Contractors) is gauged by completing a project within the stipulated contract period set by the employer and costing within the budget allowance set by the Contractor.

Regrettably, the UK has an unfortunate reputation of over-extending and overspending (Channel Tunnel, Wembley Stadium and Heathrow Terminal 5 are good examples). This cannot and is not allowed to happen on major Project overseas on the basic "threat" that if this were to happen, no further work would be given to the particular contractor in that country. Success normally generates confidence and, in turn, more projects are forthcoming to that particular Contractor.

The Projects I have contributed towards have always been completed on time (but not necessarily within budget!). The key to the success has to be:

Dedication and commitment to your work.

Continued job satisfaction and enjoyment of your chosen career.

Setting personal standards and objectives, and ensuring that they are met.

Ability to communicate with all – whatever nationality, whatever class, whatever status.

LESSONS LEARNED AND ADVICE TO OTHERS

I am strongly of the opinion that successful people are, quite simply, people who know what they want out of life! Those that have decided on a career before they leave school are far more likely to succeed and obtain job satisfaction than those who drift into a career which is not necessarily of their choosing!

This is a period where the world is becoming smaller and thereby a likelihood that many careers will either require constant overseas travel or (as in my case) permanent overseas appointments. In hindsight, lessons learned from the above are:

1. Learn a second (or third) language so communication is not an embarrassment. The unfortunate British idea "that everyone speaks English" is now long outdated.
2. Never look down to people, the ability to communicate with people at all levels of life is essential.
3. Try not to mix business with pleasure i.e. make sure you "switch off" when you leave work.
4. Always take care of your health and attempt to remain stress-free (not always possible). I still attempt to walk a minimum 10,000 steps/day (approx 4 miles), and feel good for it.

Similarly, if an individual is to consider Civil Engineering as a career, he must be prepared to:

1. Work long hours
2. Travel, meaning to live where the relevant major Project is under construction.
3. Enjoy the outdoor life!

CONCLUSIONS

- Decide what type of career suits your personal needs and ability.
- Make personal "goals" as to how you intend to develop and progress this chosen career.
- Be prepared to take knocks along the career route – i.e. the ability to overcome "bad patches" may become essential!

MAX CLIFFORD

PR Specialist & Managing Director of Max Clifford Associates

Profession/short job description:
Promotion in the media and protection from the media. I work in Public Relations with some very high profile people.

How did you make your first steps to success, and what do you consider to be the key to your success?
The key to my success was being in the right place at the right time. My first big break was when I was 19 writing a record column for a news paper. I was then head hunted by EMI to be their press officer. My first job there was to launch the Beatles. I was able to work with them closely for the first few years of their successful musical career. I have also worked with other artists such as Cliff Richard, Diana Ross and Stevie Wonder.

I had no one to teach me how to do my job; as public relations did not exist it was a totally new concept, no one would really have heard of it at this time. I left school at 15 with no qualifications and I made my own way in life. Having worked for the newspaper writing a column gave me the basics to carry on with my career. To be honest I was lucky, I was around at an amazing time of successful music.

What have been your most valuable career-defining experiences?
My most defining career experience would have been working in the EMI press office and launching the Beatles. I had only been there a few weeks and this was my first task, which turned out to be one of my biggest moments.

There have of course been others along the way such as Mohammed Ali and Frank Sinatra, but the Beatles were my starting point.

What do you wish you had known when you were younger?
I never grew up thinking if only I had known that then. I never had a plan, it all just happened. I went from pretty much nothing to the high life very quickly; staying in the best hotels, being with high profile people, flying all over the world.

So because of this I do not look back and think I wish I had known something. I learnt very quickly; starting my own business at 27 in a competitive market. I was my own boss and could learn or take nothing from anybody else, because of this.

Are there any funny / comic moments that you can remember from your career?
Hundreds and hundreds, I could go on all day as I have been doing this for 40 years now. But I shall share with you a few stories, one of which is relevant to my earlier story about the Beatles. The Marketing Director at EMI said to me once that the Beatles would be a waste of time and so not to spend too much time on them.

There are loads and loads of funny moments from my career. I deal with stars who have huge egos and they don't know how funny they are.

What advice would you have for young people just starting out in the world?
The more practical experience you get the better. So get as much experience in the area you want to be in. There is no substitute for experience. For example all the people in my office have good degrees, but they are not trained to quite the right level to fit well in my office working environment. It takes me several years to get them up to the standard I need. Having degrees and diplomas and training is all very well, and it is an invaluable tool giving you a great advantage in life but there is no substitute for experience. People that can deliver are valuable. But you will have to start hitting the ground running.

Is there anything else that you would like to add?
Follow your instincts and beliefs. This gives you the best chance in life. Stand up to be counted, it can be a mistake, you might fall back, but it makes you a better person who is nicer, happier and more rounded from this. When you are younger you can make mistakes, when you get older this is harder.

Stand up and lead. If you are lucky you can be successful and financially successful. I am, and I am so lucky and incredibly grateful.

ROSEMARY CONLEY CBE

Rosemary Conley CBE is a diet and fitness expert. She has written 30 diet books and presented 29 fitness videos/dvds with combined sales exceeding nine million copies.

The Rosemary Conley Group of companies includes Rosemary Conley Diet and Fitness Clubs, Quorn House Publishing Ltd which publishes Rosemary Conley Diet and Fitness magazine, Rosemary Conley Licences Ltd., Quorn House Media Ltd., and Rosemary Conley Enterprises.

Rosemary started her first slimming club in 1971 with an investment of £8 to print 30 posters to launch her first slimming and good grooming club. Nine years later she sold that company for £52,000.

She is an avid supporter of Young Enterprise and is President of Young Enterprise Leicestershire.

First steps to success

I found I was interested in helping people to make the most of themselves by losing weight and learning how to make the most of themselves having been on a Good Grooming Course when I was 18 years old. The rewards from seeing other people blossom was immense and is much more satisfying than just doing things to make money. The key to my success? Caring about my customer and aiming to give them the best possible service.

In my earliest years of running my slimming clubs I used to write to any member a letter of encouragement if they had gained weight. It was just a small thing but I realised the importance of it when recently, one of my own class members brought me one of those letters that I had written to her mother 30 years previously. Her mother had kept it all that time and her daughter had found it amongst some papers when she was clearing the house after her mother had died. I believe it is the little things that matter a lot in business.

Career defining experiences

Sometimes life presents you with a golden opportunity but it can be disguised as a crisis. I truly believe that all clouds have silver linings!

In 1986 I was diagnosed with a serious gallstone problem and was forced on to a low fat diet to avoid surgery. As a result of this change in my eating habits I lost a lot of inches from my hips and thighs and I realised that I had hit on something very special. I devised my own low fat diet and put it out to trial through my local radio stations - with astonishing results. Two years later my Hip and Thigh Diet became an international best seller and my career took off like a rocket.

What do I wish I had known when I was younger?

That a 'no' now, doesn't mean 'no' for ever. Perseverance is the key to success. Be nice to people and people will be nice to you. Don't ask anyone to do a job you are not prepared to do yourself and perhaps my favourite: if you have a tough job/phone call to do or make, DO IT NOW and get it out of the way.

Do I have a personal mantra?

Hold your stomach in!

Funny moments in my career?

There has been a lot of fun and laughter throughout my very privileged career but one notable occasion was when I went to Buckingham Palace to be presented with my CBE from Prince Charles in 2004. On the way to the cloakroom I fell down the stairs and my posh hat went tumbling down ahead of me. I had footmen and Royal Household staff gathering me together again rather like Humpty Dumpty. They and I thought it was hilarious!

My advice to young people starting out in the world

Be nice to people. Tell the truth. Dress smartly – people will respect you more if you do. Own up to your mistakes (everybody makes them) and be prepared to say 'sorry'. Try your best, work hard and don't be frightened of asking for help. No-one becomes successful on their own. We get there because others help us. Don't expect to be good at everything – nobody is. Play to your strengths and recognise your weaknesses and find others who have those strong points and work as a team. That's why Young Enterprise is so brilliant.

Decide on your goals and write them down. If you do, you'll achieve your dreams.

CHERIE CONCANNON

Executive Performance Coach & MD of CCC Inspirations

Chérie Concannon is an Executive Performance Coach and Managing Director of CCC Inspirations, one of the UK's leading providers of Coaching and Development. CCC Inspirations was started 18 years ago in the height of the recession and now has clients in the UK and globally.

Chérie is regarded as an expert in career progression and personal advancement at the most senior levels. Her unique, empowering six month Executive Coaching programme has been key in corporate promotion for many high level male and female clients in a large number of industries.

My First Steps to Success:
My first step to success was to make the decision to leave a highly paid, safe, employed job, taking the risk of going it alone over twenty eight years ago.

My second step to success was to identify my natural talent by making a list of all the things I was good at. No 1 was talking. I have the ability to talk on any topic in any circumstance without any 'ums' or 'ahs'. People find my ability to speak clearly and concisely very motivating and inspiring.

My third step to success was to refine my natural ability to empower people which I have achieved over the last 28 years. I've made commercial mistakes that any person who is unprepared to listen to others or take advice, when starting up, would. My key to success is perseverance undoubtedly and refusal to give up.

My Career Defining experiences:
My most valuable career defining experience was nearly going bankrupt. I faced insolvency three years into the business and this is when I began to learn my lessons. It was a terrible experience and I made a decision never to go back there.

What do I wish I had known when I was younger?
I wish I'd known when I was younger, the importance of maintaining good relationships with every human being you come into contact with. What you give out, you get back, not necessarily from the same person but you get it all back. Also I wish I'd know tattoos are like having the same poster on your bedroom wall for life!

The most valuable thing in life is to know who you are, what you stand for and be proud of it. That's the only thing that truly matters and if it takes you a whole lifetime, that's great.

My Personal Mantra:
Grab the NOW and do the best with what you have, from where you are every day.

Funny Moments in my career?
A funny moment I remember is whilst addressing a Board of Directors as part of an Executive Coaching programme, I sat down in my chair, on wheels, and I fell flat on my back with my legs up in the air. I remember the room instantly fell into complete awkward silence, then I burst into infectious laughter, it was hilarious.

My advice to young people just starting out in the world:

- Be brave
- Do everything you can to find out what your talent is and make use of it. I believe everyone has a natural talent and if you can find out what it is and make the most of it, you'll be successful.
- Build the best support network you can; professionally and personally.
- Never allow yourself to get bored.
- Laugh everyday.
- Always have a passion in your life.
- Be excited and enthusiastic.
- Get to know yourself inside out, how you think, feel and operate.
- Think of the world as a very small place.
- Take care of your body, it has to last you a while.

www.cccinspirations.com

DAVID FLETCHER

Art Valuer and Auctioneer

I am an auctioneer and valuer of Fine Art and Antiques, even though, somewhat confusingly, I qualified many years ago as a Chartered Surveyor. Although I once operated a theodolite, and occasionally measured up the odd cottage in order to identify the existence of a 'flying freehold' (that part of a property that overhangs the lower floor of an adjoining property) I never really liked surveying. However becoming a Chartered Surveyor fulfilled two very important objectives. Firstly it meant that I was a professional. Secondly it meant that I had a career. Having a career meant that I could earn a living.

The need for school leavers to 'get a qualification' was of overriding importance to the schoolmasters who had successfully brought us to the threshold of adulthood. A qualification guaranteed a career and in those days having a career ensured that you had a job for life. The terrible uncertainties that had dogged the young lives of my teachers' generation, thrown, just as their own fathers had been, into the maelstrom of world war, doubtless fuelled this desire that their sons should find stability in their own lives. For this reason I am loathe, even now, to criticize this mindset and certainly I went along with it at the time. My favourite subject was art and I must say that the thought of three or four years at art school in 1970s London seemed particularly attractive, but my art master, Ron Dalzell, told me emphatically that I was not good enough to draw, paint or sculpt professionally, so that was that – I decided to become a Chartered Surveyor.

Actually, it wasn't quite as simple as that. I liked the countryside and had even thought about farming as a career. Working as a land agent at Sandringham or Blenheim Palace rather appealed to me and one way of becoming a land agent was to train in the appropriate division of the Royal Institution of Chartered Surveyors and this I duly did. Having failed my exams at college, I qualified with Peacocks, an old fashioned and gentlemanly firm of estate agents, auctioneers and land agents based in Bedford. In due course I was put on the rostrum, or more exactly, asked to stand on an old chair, from which I conducted my first auction sale.

This, unsurprisingly, was not in the least bit grand, but I was young and it was all very exciting.

Never having had a 'career plan', things evolved in a typically unstructured manner, helped somewhat by an uncharacteristically risky move to Hertfordshire where I took a saleroom manager's job, for which, in all truth, I was woefully ill prepared. For a time I blagged things like mad, but ultimately found my feet. Since those long off and fondly remembered days, I have worked for several firms, including Phillips (now Bonhams), the international Fine Art Auctioneers, and now run my own business in Bedford. Happily, and to give my career symmetry, I act as a consultant to Peacocks, where it all started nearly 40 years ago

I have hugely enjoyed my work. I have met a great many intelligent, likable and amusing people who have been clients or colleagues and have often become friends. I have earned very little, but I learned a lot.

There is a real thrill to be had in taking the rostrum to conduct a big auction sale. The auctioneer knows what reserve (the price below which an item, or group of items, will not be sold), has been placed on each lot. He, or she, also knows if any 'commission' (i.e. absentee) bids have been left, but beyond that things are largely unpredictable. The saleroom is a combination of theatre and the dealing floor.

However it is the process of cataloguing that I have enjoyed most and the acquisition of a 'hands-on' knowledge of the fine and decorative arts that has given me the greatest buzz. I think I know the difference between a Kentian interior and one that might have been designed by Robert Adam. I know the difference between a soft paste porcelain figure and a one made of hard paste and I know the difference between a period Chippendale chair and an Edwardian copy. I do not necessarily know the difference between a Carracci and a Caravaggio, but then that is not my field and, in any case, I know someone who does.

When I reflect about what I wish I had known at the age of eighteen, I must admit that most of the hazards about which I was blissfully unaware have turned out to be pretty obvious. Firstly I would mention that, whatever your age, life has its challenges. When one is young there somehow seems more time to face up to these, and the consequences of not doing so seem less significant than they later become. I certainly never imagined that what was a period of four weeks in 1969 would have shrunk to a day or two by 1999.

If I had known this I would have squared up to matters more quickly, would have spent a little less time in pubs, taken more holidays and probably have been a bit richer. I might even have written 'that' book which, as they say, everyone has inside them.

Eighteen year olds never really worry about money – why should they? I do not like to strike a negative note but I am being honest to my brief when I say that I wish I had known that the future was going to be just a little more difficult than I assumed it would be. Certainly, it would have helped if I had known a little about the stock market, building societies and how to obtain a mortgage. I did not even know the difference between a current account and a deposit account. Also I wish that I had been aware that my pension would not fund itself. As I mentioned above, time flies by at an alarming rate. I do not want to frighten the reader but believe me - you will be fifty eight much sooner than you think, and very near to drawing your own pension!

A good education brings you the qualifications you need, and a good school like Bedford will churn out self confident and sophisticated young people by the thousand. I am a great believer in a laid back approach to life and much admire that easy going attitude, sometimes dismissed as 'casualness', that was associated with Bedford School in my day. Of course it meant that a few students who should have gone on to play county cricket or international rugby never did, but it ensured that they were good people who wore their talents with modesty, and took their occasional failures at the crease (and in life) with Kiplingesque grace. I am no fan of 'self assertiveness' courses and, given the choice, prefer non-confrontational people, but for all that, I wish that I had learned to be a bit more pushy.

I believe that in business, as in life, you need to be affable - there is no point in making enemies. Getting worked up about things is also pretty useless, although you should always ask yourself why they have happened. It is also important to 'be up for it' – it is far better to say 'yes' and worry about how you are going to do what you have just committed yourself to, than never to have the chance to find out. Above all, I think that you should be inquisitive or you will never learn anything that someone else hasn't chosen to tell you. I have found that an amazing amount of people simply do not have enquiring minds, preferring, instead the 'parrot fashion' method of learning.

So that's it – whether I would have done anything differently or whether you, having read this will do so, is an entirely different matter.

SADIE FROST

Actress & Clothes Designer

Profession/short job description:
I am an actress and clothes designer.

How did you make your first steps to success, and what do you consider to be the key to your success?
I enrolled in acting, dancing and singing lessons when I was 10 years old and got a scholarship to the Italia Conti stage school in London. I consider the key to success to be perseverance, hard work and professionalism.

What have been your most valuable career-defining experiences?
Working with great directors such as Francis Ford Coppola and Nicolas Hyntner. Being brave enough to accept a one woman show and put 150% into it.

What do you wish you had known when you were younger?
When I was younger I wish I had been more confident and didn't listen to my inner demons. I don't think I realised how much hard work can improve your talents

Do you have a personal Mantra
Before I go out on stage I say to myself "breathe in love, breathe out fear".

Are there any funny / comic moments that you can remember from your career?
There are many funny moments! Recently i found myself on stage with a very drunk and difficult woman who was ruining the performance for both the audience and myself. I had to think quickly and professionally on how to continue the show. I asked her to leave!

What advice would you have for young people just starting out in the world?
Be focused and dedicated. Try to think about the future and what you really want to do.

ADAM HART-DAVIS

Scientist, Author, Photographer, Historian & Broadcaster

Profession/short job description:
I am freelance – that is I have no permanent job, and therefore no salary. I depend on people asking me to do things and then paying me for it. I write books and articles, I present radio and television programmes and I take photographs; so I describe myself as a writer, photographer, and broadcaster.

How did you make your first steps to success, and what do you consider to be the key to your success?
When I left school (with A-levels in physics, chemistry, and maths) I had no idea what I wanted to do with my life, and I still have not decided what to do when I grow up. I went to university, because my brother had done that, and was then asked to do a DPhil, so I drifted along.

Five years later I could not get a job at university, and I dropped out into publishing, editing science books for the Oxford University Press. That was fun, but a bit slow, and five years later I went to Yorkshire Television as a researcher in the science department.

I was a researcher for six years, a producer for eleven years, and then I got on the wrong side of the camera, and became a presenter. In 1993 I left Yorkshire Television, and have been freelance ever since.

I decided when I was about 35 that I was never going to earn a big salary; so I should start earning royalties as well, and I began to take serious photographs and to write articles and books. The photography was successful quite quickly, and the writing grew steadily; I now earn more money from writing than from anything else. The keys to my success? I write easily and clearly (even if my prose is not exciting), I take competent photographs and learn from my many mistakes, and I speak clearly, with a knack of making science and technology understandable.

What have been your most valuable career-defining experiences?
Being allowed to produce the tv series "Arthur C Clarke's World Of Strange Powers", being able to invent and produce the educational series "Scientific Eye", and being able to present my own programmes, starting with "Local Heroes".

What do you wish you had known when you were younger?
That you don't have to choose a career for life while you are still in your teens – or even twenties.

Do you have a personal Mantra?
Try to get more young people, especially girls, into science and engineering. When all is gloom and doom, always find something positive to look forward to.

What advice would you have for young people just starting out in the world?
Stick with it. Remember Charles Darwin spent years and years studying and accumulating information, before he changed the world for ever.

Is there anything else that you would like to add?
Good luck – and don't panic if you don't have a life plan. Just seize any opportunities that come your way.

MARGARET HEFFERNAN

Entrepreneur & Writer

How did you make your first steps to success, and what do you consider to be the key to your success?

The first steps I took were not to success, because I took a low level job when (I realize) now I could have aimed much higher. However, I joined a good company- the BBC- and was able to find better opportunities within it. So I'd say the first key to success is Work with good people. If you find yourself in a poor company with mediocre people-get out!

Other smart things I did: make it clear that you are ambitious. You can't expect people to know if you don't tell them (especially if you're a female!). Most people will help if they can- they just don't know what you need. Ask for help. Get as much experience and training as you can. Volunteer for demanding projects- especially new projects where there may not be such entrenched people or processes and where you may be able to create a space for yourself to shine.Develop a sterling reputation. Everyone you meet will form an opinion of you. Make sure it is a good one. Britain is a small island and a bad reputation will follow you everywhere. Every email you don't answer, any phone call you don't return, will be remembered by someone. I'm shocked to discover that a good proportion of my success can be attributed to nothing more fancy than plain good manners. Ask questions. Curiosity is how you learn; curious people tend to know more than uncurious people. When you ask questions, you learn things from the horse's mouth. The only reason not to ask questions is because you know everything. I haven't reached that stage yet and probably you haven't either.

Finally I'd say of myself, and have heard many other highly successful people say the same thing: be prepared to take risks. Not stupid risks but smart ones. When I look back, my biggest achievements have derived from a willingness to turn off the path and try something new.

What have been your most valuable career-defining experiences?

Certainly being fired was career-defining experience and a very frightening one. But almost every successful person has been fired (at least once) so the important thing is not what has happened but how you respond and what you learn from it. There is no success without failure- so success has as much to do with resilience as anything else. Yell, scream, cry- and then get on with it.

Two other related thoughts:

1. I was once producing a show for BBC2 and, very close to the broadcast date, realised there was a mistake in it. Fixing it would cost time and money but I did so- because I reckoned that you should never, ever settle for something you aren't proud of, as long as there is some opportunity to fix it. I still believe that: if you have any opportunity to make something better, you have to take it.

2. A boss once asked me to lie and I did. I would never EVER do that again. It was a mistake which I made because I was very young- it was my first job- and I didn't want him to think I was a prig. But it was the wrong thing to do.

What do you wish you had known when you were younger?

- That people remember you rather more than you imagine- so everything counts!
- That just doing the basics well carries a lot of weight. Being on time, on budget, doing what you say you will do, delivering on promises, setting appropriate expectation- none of these sound earth-shattering but they are worth their weight in gold. I know plenty of outstanding business people who attribute their success to one thing only: they always did what they said they' do.
- I wish I'd known how good I was and taken my career more seriously.
- You can almost always negotiate and even if you lose, people respect you more because you tried.
- Don't lose touch with people you like- especially if you are in the midst of failure.

What advice would you have for young people just starting out in the world of business?

- Remember that business is one way you can change the world- by treating people well, building great products, giving great service, treating everyone with respect.
- Money is important but it isn't the only important thing.
- Power is about being able to provide- it isn't about ordering people around. The more you can give people, the more power you have to make the world a better place.
- Always try to do work you love. Even if you're in an uninspiring job, try to find something in it that develops you as a person. There's always something…

Is there anything else that you would like to add?

The best companies have all kinds of different people in them. The reason for this is because, the greater the variety of people, the more ideas, information and insight they will bring to problem- solving. So always try to be around people who are different from you, who know other things than the things you know, who have different backgrounds and experiences. You will learn more and life will be a lot more interesting!
Good luck!

JOHN HOOPER

Construction surveyor / estimator

Profession/short job description:
I am a construction surveyor/ estimator. I own a small consultancy practice, mainly negotiating new contracts for contractors and developers.

How did you make your first steps to success, and what do you consider to be the key to your success?
I started applying the same energy to business as I had to sport. I learnt the business and pitfalls, became as knowledgeable and efficient as brainpower limitations allowed, made and maintained useful contacts, allowing me eventually to set up my own practice.

What have been your most valuable career-defining experiences?
Having an excellent mentor/ role model in early years- I learnt a huge amount in that period and it wasn't in the text books!

I used that knowledge to aid two smallish companies to become very successful, again learning from the entrepreneurship and calculated risk- taking of the owners. Ironically, while this made me a director, it also resulted in redundancy as the (now) millionaire owners sold up… but also provided the impetus to "go it alone".

What do you wish you had known when you were younger?
To look at the broader picture, beyond just ensuring the mortgage can be paid- it's easy to be stuck in that groove.

To seek out opportunities rather than awaiting their fortuities arrival (or not).

What advice would you have for young people just starting out in the world of business?
Review as many prospects or options as possible and in which you have a genuine interest. Speak to the best people in those fields before deciding on your course of actions. i.e do your research.

If you have a great product idea, patent it before you even tell your grandma. Make sure you work with the best available, treat them with respect and kindness- they will need motivation (not necessarily just money) to help you make a success of your career and, potentially, your fortune.. oh, and have fun!

Is there anything else that you would like to add?
Luck will always play some part; if it about being in the right place at the right time.
Take advice from good and experienced people but always think for yourself.

Believe in yourself, you can do it.

RAPEEPAN LUANGARAMRUT

Thai Celeb

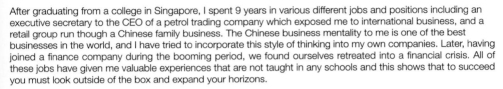

How did you make the first steps to success, and what do you consider to be the key to your success?
Since a young age I have always wanted to be an entrepreneur. As a result I have always been determined to learn as much as possible from each business that I have worked in, in order to develop in depth my understanding of business and more importantly business networking which I think is the significant factor in facilitating any business success. Every business step has given me more determination and each piece of experience I have gained has developed me.

After graduating from a college in Singapore, I spent 9 years in various different jobs and positions including an executive secretary to the CEO of a petrol trading company which exposed me to international business, and a retail group run though a Chinese family business. The Chinese business mentality to me is one of the best businesses in the world, and I have tried to incorporate this style of thinking into my own companies. Later, having joined a finance company during the booming period, we found ourselves retreated into a financial crisis. All of these jobs have given me valuable experiences that are not taught in any schools and this shows that to succeed you must look outside of the box and expand your horizons.

I then decided that I was ready to start my own business, but one that does not require a large initial fund. My choice was to be a construction contractor. The key reason for this was that I could rent equipments from my parents who were themselves construction contractors. It turned out to be a great success for me and luckily there were quite a few opportunities that fell onto my lap. The government, under the directorship of General Prem Tinsulanont, was planning the new development of Eastern Seaboard, supposedly the nation's largest industrial estate as well as a commercial port. I was invited to be a consultant to many of the world's largest multinational firms from England, Belgium, Netherlands, Norway, and Malaysia, who were all looking to invest in Eastern Seaboard. Some of these firms decided to publically list themselves in the Thailand stock exchange, and invited me to sit on their board committee and audit committee, roles which I still hold for several firms.

Which attribute do you regard as key to your success?
I always learn everything I can from industries and people around me and I strongly believe in learning from others. Even as a successful entrepreneur myself I still feel that there is much more for me to learn. Sincerity is also the key to success. I take pride in always treating people with respect and care regardless of their power, wealth, and position. I guess this is the key to my success in all professions and social contexts.

What do you wish you had known when you were younger?
At a young age, seeing what my parents had to do for their business day in day out it felt unbearable. For example, waiting to see a client, waking up before dawn, working through lunch, paying respect to people, and even cooking for workers just seemed to me over the top and unnecessary work. However, I came to realise later that I unknowingly inherited those valuable characteristics from my parents and they made become who I am today. You must push yourself if you want to achieve.

Do you have a personal mantra?
Once I set my mind to do something, I will do all I can to achieve the best results.

Are there any funny/ comic moments that you can remember from your career?
As a consultant to many multinational firms, I was invited to attend a party held by a firm in England. I meticulously bought the nicest dresses I could think of for the party made out of the finest linen with exquisite broidery. It turned out that the dress I wore was totally inappropriate for the weather; I looked funny in the party and also caught a cold.

What advice would you have for young people just starting out in the world?

Nowadays, children are brought up totally differently from my time, in particular being open minded and listening to different ideas. Many are fixated on developing their own ideas and creating their own career path as it gives them more pride and independence. Nevertheless, I just hope that they are open minded enough to consider the businesses their parents have diligently established and bring their innovation and new technology to help develop more sustainable business for their family.

Also, younger generations rarely adhere to old traditions and relentlessly seek new opportunities and ideas which I think is a good thing. However, some may make the mistake of abandoning things every time they feel bored or lose interest. Strong determination in sticking to the goal from the start through to completion is an old expression that I still believe is a key ingredient of success for all people.

ANA MARIA PACHECO

World renowned artist

Following two degrees I had to take the decision on whether to make a career in music or visual art. I chose the latter and began to work as an artist and my first step was to get involved in exhibitions of national relevance. Subsequently, I received a British Council Scholarship to study at the Slade School of Fine Art in London and this was probably my career-defining experience.

Often people feel they wished to have had more knowledge when they were younger. It is impossible for me to know what I would have wished to have known because I have no regrets and what I have achieved is through experience.

Young people must keep in mind that the idea of success is not so much about material or financial gain but more about being able to succeed in what one proposes to do in life. To achieve success the most important thing is to maintain the integrity between thought and action, to transform ones potential into actuality, and to work hard to sustain a continual intellectual curiosity.

IAN PECK

Chartered Surveyor, Bidwells

Profession / short job description:
I am a Chartered Surveyor and a partner in Bidwells which is the 15th largest property consultancy in the United Kingdom.

I played rugby for Bedford, Cambridge University and England in 1979 and I played cricket for Cambridge University and Northampton County Cricket Club.

How did you make your first steps to success and what do you consider to be the key to your success?
A single minded passion combined with hard work, good training and mentoring.

What have been your most valuable career-defining experiences?
Interesting question: I cannot name a specific time: it has tended to be trial and error.

What do you wish you had known when you were younger?
A better understanding of career options, what they offer in terms of job satisfaction and financially. I did not really appreciate what I could do with my life professionally and therefore I had nothing to home in on.

How and when to confront difficult issues would be another point. Problems tend not to go away and if left, they only get worse and bigger with time.

The use of language and the importance of articulating a compelling argument is important.

Do you have a personal mantra?
Well a few spring to mind but there is nothing I follow religiously.

"What goes around comes around", so be nice to people on the way up because you might well meet them again on the way down. So treat people properly.

Core values are important; such as honesty, integrity, hard work, play hard and treat people properly. The world around you will change constantly but core values always stay the same. Professionally, integrity is incredibly important.

Are there any funny / comic moments that you can remember from your career?
Pretty much my entire career, but no particular moments. Being able to laugh at oneself is better than laughing at others all the time as this can keep you very amused most of the time.

What advice would you have for young people just starting out in the world?
Get out there. Pursue what you are interested in and go that extra mile to achieve it. You cannot excel in something you are not passionate about. Be focused on your aim, and focus intently on what you want to achieve. It does not have to be something complex, it can be something simple as you will achieve either way. To get that focus you need passion. I have mainly observed a lot of this focus from friends who have also done well.

If you want to be a leader, then lead from the front not the back. You have to practise what you preach and lead by example. Have a clear view and select good people around you to help you achieve it.

VLADIMIR RAPIC

Hairstylist

Vladimir Rapic hairstylist born in eastern Europe in a country formerly known as Yugoslavia. Based in a Mayfair salon (Steven Carey) but working around the world – fashion shoots, music videos, playing with famous people and royals......

I arrived in London in 1992 with a hundred pounds to my name, very basic English and a desire to succeed. I was trained by a top stylist in Belgrade for two years working six days a week and going to college for five of those as well. It was hard but I knew what I wanted. I was a lazy but bright and artistic child. Ultimately I knew I wanted to work in something creative but enterprising. Hair was the answer. It could take me anywhere in the world potentially.

I chose London but before I got here I had some thinking to do and some obligations. A year in the army came first followed by a year of going to university to please my parents. These didn't work out for any parties involved! As the war started in the former Yugoslavia I packed my bags, headed west and followed hairdressing.

London was a big city – no family, no friends and a lot of fear but hey, look at me now telling you that you can do it yourselves. Just being good at a profession however is not enough, especially today in the world of big brands, big names and lots of competition. You need to develop a strategy and a persona that will mark you out. This means working on things other than the core professional skills. I'm talking about customer service, widening the horizons for you and your customers, keeping it fun and interesting. For me this has meant keeping informed, travelling, working in different languages, curiosity about other cultures and following the arts and trends. All these make you stand out in a crowded market of equally talented people.

With time, maturity and lots of hard work this has added up to giving me the choice of where, with whom and how hard I want to work. I've never chosen to have my own shop or my name on a brand but I am the product. People come to me, they recommend me and they know what my name brings. It is a high standard every time, it's entertaining and it can be bold enough to explore a look and a confidence they didn't think they had. That's more than a haircut.

VLADIMIR RAPIC – for Steven Carey
112 Mount Street
Mayfair
London
W1K 2TU

MALCOLM ROSE

Author

I murdered two people yesterday. That's the beauty of being a fiction writer. A novelist can do anything, be anyone, and go anywhere because it all happens in the imagination. I am a great musician, the best footballer in the land, a devious murderer, the world's leading detective, a very bright girl, and many other characters.

I used to be told off at school for daydreaming. Now, I make my living from it. I have the best job in the known universe because I am a professional daydreamer.

I was born in Coventry in 1953 and began writing stories as a hobby while taking a PhD in chemistry at York University. It was my escape from real life and I did not consider publishing anything. It was my girlfriend (now wife) who suggested that I ought to try and get a novel published. I had never thought of writing as anything other than a fun hobby. Anyway, she nagged me for five years before I dared to send off a manuscript to a publisher. My first novel was published in 1985.

I carried on my career in science because I loved investigating things. I became a Lecturer in Chemistry at several universities but the job left very little time for writing fiction, so I did it mostly after midnight. Perhaps that's why people say my strongest scenes are set on dark nights! But there are only 24 hours in a day and I could not cram two careers into them. I put aside my test-tubes in 1996 and became a full-time writer of thrillers and crime stories for young people. I guess I gave up my job in science because I felt more special as a novelist and because of the freedom that comes with being a freelance writer. I have now published 36 novels.

Many people think it strange and fascinating that a scientist should also be a novelist. I don't. Scientists have to be creative and patient to carry out research and they need to write up their work in articles and textbooks. Novelists have to be imaginative and persistent and they need to be nifty with a pen and paper. The requirements are similar. I used to add chemicals together, brew them up a bit and investigate what happened, but now I mix fictional characters, stir in a bit of conflict and investigate what happens. Hopefully, either can be colourful or even explosive.

I wish I'd realized – or someone better informed had told me – when I was at school that writing a story is an investigation. Then I would have taken more interest in writing fiction when I was at school. But I didn't. All my writing was self-taught later.

I guess my books are classed mainly as thrillers or crime stories. I enjoy myself most when the story has a basis in modern science. Most of my crime fiction is awash with the gruesome forensic science that lurks behind police investigations. My thrillers are frequently fuelled by science as well: chemical and biological warfare, environmental clashes, cloning, medical advances, weather manipulation, and so on. Because science is always advancing, it provides an endless source of ideas for a novelist. I don't always exploit my scientific background when I'm writing fiction but I often tap into it for the odd plot.

My books are not anti-science. I use science in them to solve problems. The conflict comes from misuse of science through the corrupting effect of money, politics, the military and religion.

I get ideas from several places: newspaper and magazine articles, the lyrics of music I always listen to – the louder the better – when I'm writing, and my own interests in science, sport and so on. I write only about topics that make me passionate. Frequently, I am motivated by outrage. The use of chemistry and biology to kill people in warfare, racism, bullying, new weapon development and several other pet hates have been perverse inspiration. I am not sufficiently naive that I believe I can solve big problems by writing a novel about them, but at least I can raise awareness. That is one of my main aims: to make a reader think while he or she is being entertained. And that is why I write for young people. The young have open minds that are receptive to new ideas – probably more so than boring old adults!

If I'm asked to pass on tips to young writers, I tell them to try the writing tips on my website (www.malcolmrose.co.uk). As far as publishing is concerned, I ask them to be patient. I think young writers should simply enjoy writing, push themselves and thereby get even better, read widely, and gain life experiences that will inform their future writing. This might even include taking a job or developing other interests and afterwards using the experience in their writing.

It was hard to get a novel published when I first did it in the 1980s. Sadly, it's harder now. It's always possible to post novels on the Internet but the best way of getting published today is to get a literary agent first. They are listed in The Writers' and Artists' Yearbook and a good agent is a massive help to a writer and a massive step towards publication.

Because it's not easy to get a book published, the new writer needs to develop a thick skin. Get used to criticism and rejection slips! Getting rejected doesn't turn a good story into a bad one. It just means it hasn't yet found the publisher who loves it. This is where my motto comes in. I repeat it a lot. It comes in handy when you begin to question if you're any good at doing something. OF COURSE YOU CAN DO IT. And, yes, Barack Obama did steal it off me for his Presidential campaign.

DR. MICHAEL SKINNER

Senior Lecturer & Head of Vaccine Vector Group, Imperial College London

Why did you choose Virology as your chosen field?
I was fascinated by infectious diseases, particularly those that we would now call 'emerging diseases', many of which were caused by viruses. At the time it was a good way to move into the then newly-developing field of molecular biology. It was also clear that many discoveries in the way the normal cell worked came from the use of viruses to perturb the normal workings of the cell, an intellectual approach that appealed to me as my PhD had made much use of genetics (i.e. mutations) to achieve a similar goal (but at that time methods for manipulating the host cell genome were not even rudimentary).

What are, in your opinion, the advantages of being a scientist?
Intellectual challenge. Being at the cutting edge of knowledge. Seeing something for the first time that nobody else has ever seen!

Academic freedom. The ability to interact with scientists from all cultures and countries.

Passing on the passion and excitement I have for my subject to young new scientists and to members of the public, young and old (including school pupils).
Travel and good opportunities to work abroad.

What are, in your opinion, the disadvantages of being a scientist?
Extreme difficulties and uncertainties in becoming 'established' in the career.
Financial compensation is considerably less than intellectual peers in other sectors.

What advice would you give for young people just starting out in the world of science (particularly Biology)?
- Don't be afraid to ask questions - you won't look silly!
- Read around enough to work out what aspects interest you most - prepare explanations of why they interest you and practice them on friends or acquaintances.
- Keep up with new developments. Publish and get used to writing grant applications.
- Is there anything else that you would like to add?
- Establishing an academic career in science is tough. You have to be self-motivated and hard working as well as having scientific curiosity. You have to be open to criticism and adept at self-criticism. You should be critical of what you read and hear. You need to think logically. It is an elitist career, though your background should not be an issue. I should say that my answers refer to academic and government-funded science, not the commercial sector, of which I have no personal experience

> Trust your gut, don't be afraid to
> value yourself and trust your instincts

Billy Mann

Music

Music

Many people are interested in taking up music as a career however to become a professional in this field takes dedication and perseverance. Although becoming successful is very hard work, the glamour associated with music attracts many into this field. The music industry is extremely diverse and employs not only the musicians themselves but also offers other careers such as sound technicians, producers, vocal coaches and A&R (Artist and Repertoire) executives, the people responsible for scouting new talent and developing them into profitable artists.

Although a lot of hard work is needed, many find music to be an extremely enjoyable field to pursue in their lives.

Concert Pianist

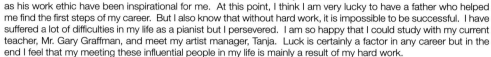

How did you make your first steps to success, and what do you consider to be the key to your success?

I grew up in a musical family. My father is one of the leading composers in China and as a child I was constantly surrounded by his music. The creative novelty of his music as well as his work ethic have been inspirational for me. At this point, I think I am very lucky to have a father who helped me find the first steps of my career. But I also know that without hard work, it is impossible to be successful. I have suffered a lot of difficulties in my life as a pianist but I persevered. I am so happy that I could study with my current teacher, Mr. Gary Graffman, and meet my artist manager, Tanja. Luck is certainly a factor in any career but in the end I feel that my meeting these influential people in my life is mainly a result of my hard work.

What have been your most valuable career-defining experiences?

Every concert experience is different and therefore valuable. Sometimes, I feel excited and happy on the way to a concert or on stage, but I just as often feel lonely and nervous. But no matter how I feel, I always enjoy my concerts and try to pay attention to how I feel each time before I play. The concert atmosphere inevitably produces an intense experience that is difficult to duplicate in a practice room, and each concert allows me to better understand myself and the composers whose music I play. I cherish each experience and collectively they are one of my inspirations.

What do you wish you had known when you were younger?

I started piano lessons very early and was privileged to attend the elementary and middle school divisions of the Shanghai Conservatory of Music, so musically I don't think I could have done much better. However, I do wish I had been exposed to more modern music earlier, my father's music aside. I only began listening to more 20th and 21st century music when I entered Curtis. More generally, in music and in any field, I think it is good to expose oneself to as broad a range of things as possible early.

Do you have a personal Mantra?

Not really, because my career and my playing are in a constant state of change. I don't have one rule or philosophy to cover everything; however, I have always believed that to stop developing is to stop being an artist.

Are there any funny / comic moments that you can remember from your career?

I am a serious musician and I am very involved in every concert I have participated in. I do enjoy travelling to different places and meeting different people.

What advice would you have for young people just starting out in the world of music?

It is very hard to have a career as a classical musician. You have to start serious practicing when you are very young in order to build up necessary facility, and when you get older you have to learn to always raise your standards and maintain concentration and focus on your playing even with all the concertizing.

Is there anything else that you would like to add?

The abundance of emotional content in classical music and the richness of the experience it provides make it worth the patience required to become familiarized enough to appreciate it. I hope more young people will give it a chance -- it is well worth it!

ELIO LEONI-SCETI

CEO of EMI Music

Mr Leoni-Sceti, 42, was born and educated in Rome and started his career in 1988 as a brand manager at Procter & Gamble before moving to Reckitt Benckiser in 1992 as a category manager. Mr Leoni-Sceti hails from consumer goods company Reckitt Benckiser, whose products include Dettol, Nurofen and Finish dishwasher powder.

In the last seven years before joining EMI as CEO in September 2008, he has been an Executive Vice President at Reckitt Benckiser and a key player in the growth of the company. From 2001 to 2005, he was Head of Category Development, leading the company's innovation, product pipeline, global marketing and media and, since 2005, he has been Reckitt Benckiser's Head of Europe, a £3 billion business which has seen outstanding levels of growth under his leadership

My current Job is CEO of EMI music. EMI is one of the 4 historical Music "major labels", and was recently bought and made private by Terra Firma. The CEO of a company is the person who is ultimately responsible to set the company vision and strategy, set the targets for the company and prioritize the available human & financial resources to achieve these goals.

This job is the last step of a very international career that has taken me to live in 7 countries and to work - with alternating responsibilities - over more than 40.. I'm mentioning this because the international profile of the companies I've worked with in the last 20 years (Procter and Gamble; Benckiser; Reckitt Benckiser; EMI), and the personal life experience associated with working in various countries, was instrumental in opening my mind, and it has been a key asset for my career as it developed.

An important attitude, which i found helpful as my career progressed, has always been about the focus and determination to "do your job" - whichever that job is at that time - at best. What this means is simply to keep the energy and 100% attention on what one person is doing at that time: the project, the opportunity, or the challenge that needed to be addressed for my current job, and not get distracted with other things, like the next career step, internal company politics, or secondary objectives... and importantly, you get a real kick out of succeeding at what you are doing, just for your own pleasure and not (just) for others to see how good you are, Self-motivation has always worked for me, and is a key characteristic many industry leaders share.

So, what worked for me was to keep the large majority, if not all, of my focus on winning/succeeding at what i was doing at that given moment in time, and to do it for the pleasure of seeing the results of the effort/work myself, for my own satisfaction. I found out that - if you work for a good company (the most important choice to make is this one, from the very start!) - and you consistently succeed at what you are doing, then you'll be given opportunities to grow and to develop. The reason is simply that real human talent is a truly scarce resource, and proving with attitude and results to be a "talent" won't go un-noticed.

What do I wish I had known when I was younger?

Probably how important it is to chose a "mentor" in both your life and career as you grow up. The mentor figure is a fundamental one for each of us; I believe however at the time it is a difficult need to recognise, when we are young we all tend to believe "we don't need a mentor", or that the one that life (or your company..) offers to you doesn't really work (too old for me, too young for that, too different from me, too.. etc). Reality is that a mentor (could be a parent, a friend, your boss, or whoever you respect and could learn from) is a key part of our development, and choosing the right one can make a substantial difference. How to chose the right one is a very long story.. for another day.. but in essence it must be someone that inspires you to better yourself.. someone "you want to be like" as you grow up: If you see one.. grab him/her!

One last thing:

A good career, possibly for any job type, is a journey and not a destination. A good job, or a good career, really never ends, and when it does you should be surprised that it did. Planning for an end point to a successful career might work for some, but i haven't met many successful people that planned it like this.

If you are good at it, and you enjoy the ride, there is always more of it to go for!

BILLY MANN

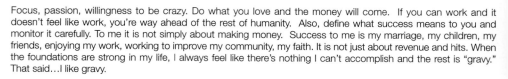

President of A&R-Labels International, EMI Music President of Global Artist Management, EMI Music Songwriter, Record Producer, Artist Manager

How did you make your first steps to success and what do you consider to be the key to your success?

Never give up and when you find a believer, a mentor, a fan, a teacher that connects with you: Cherish them. These people will help you and enjoy your growth and being part of it. For any artist the mantra should be "fans first." Cherish your fans, however few or many; from your parents to your friend, you must super-serve them.

Focus, passion, willingness to be crazy. Do what you love and the money will come. If you can work and it doesn't feel like work, you're way ahead of the rest of humanity. Also, define what success means to you and monitor it carefully. To me it is not simply about making money. Success to me is my marriage, my children, my friends, enjoying my work, working to improve my community, my faith. It is not just about revenue and hits. When the foundations are strong in my life, I always feel like there's nothing I can't accomplish and the rest is "gravy." That said...I like gravy.

What have been your most valuable career-defining experiences?

I think in life there are those who are defined by events and those who define themselves in spite of events and challenges. I think that if your core is strong – your self-worth, your values, the people in your life who love you and have your back, you can overcome the greatest obstacles and odds. Don't be defined by others or events, define yourself among the rest. If I could pick one career defining experience it would be when a major recording artist (who I thought was a close friend) took advantage of me in the earlier part of my career and "land-grabbed" royalties from me without asking. Unfortunately, this happens in many businesses, but this was a "friend" – at least so I thought, and it was hard to digest. A year later that same artist asked me to write and produce for their greatest hits record which would have meant a great financial opportunity for me. My wife was pregnant with our second child and anyone in the business would have killed for the chance both financially and musically. But I turned it down. I turned it down because working with someone--no matter how famous and successful--who didn't value me was not something I could let myself do. Everyone told me I was crazy to walk away from the money and, to be honest, for about three weeks I thought I was crazy, too. But I felt good. I was right. I did the right thing. A month later, I met Pink (AKA Alecia Moore) and she and I went on to sell over 10 million albums together and write hits like "God is a DJ", Stupid Girls" and "Dear Mr President." Value yourself, respect others and others will value and respect you.

What do you wish you had known when you were younger?

I wish I had known less and lived a more innocent childhood.

Do you have a personal Mantra?

True North: life is a direction not a location.

Are there any funny / comic moments that you can remember from your career?

Too many to single out one. But here's a vision: driving 20 hours in a van to play a 20 minute acoustic set at a Hard Rock Café in San Antonio, Texas while the family in the front table (yes, they were eating burgers) were yelling out, "More ketchup!" to the waitress. Ahhhh...humility.

What advice would you have for young people just starting out in the world of business?

Do what you love and the money will come.

Is there anything else that you would like to add?

Trust your gut, don't be afraid to value yourself and trust your instincts.

DOUGLAS MERRILL

When I was asked to write a few pages giving advice to 18 year olds, first I choked with anxiety: What do I have to tell 18 year olds today? But then I thought about it, looked around at the 18 to 22 year olds I know, and recognized there are three themes I wish I had known. First, don't worry about your whole life now – you will get a chance to change course later. Second, relationships matter more than you think they do. Finally, value diversity, relationships with people who aren't like you.

When I was 18, I, along with most of my peers, thought that life would flow in front of me like a motorway, running straight in the direction I chose at University. My major would determine my career, and so forth. Most of the people who started University with me spent a great deal of time, effort, and anxiety selecting a major, which would determine their careers. Because they spent so much time and effort selecting a major, there would be no surprises for them, they believed their lives were all planned out. That turns out to be false, in almost all cases. Generally speaking, people change careers every 7 years. Over my work life, I've been a professor, a researcher, a financial planner, a consultant, and entrepreneur, a technologist, and an executive coach. No selection of major could have prepared me for all of these careers.

You can't predict future changes, so you shouldn't worry so much about trying to do so. Rather, try to get yourself ready for a long and windy road over your life. How do you prepare for such a journey? You build a solid sense of direction, the ability to take curves smoothly, and a confidence in your ability to drive the road.

I'm not saying that you shouldn't have goals. Goals are great, they help you separate life's wheat from its chaff. They give you that sense of direction and help you learn interesting things. No, please form goals, just recognize that your goals will change. In fact, sometimes they will change radically, and that's good. You should learn to react to changes.

You can learn to react by giving yourself a very broad education. It's too early to be overly specific – learn everything. In university, I majored in reading, more or less. I got degrees in sociology and philosophy, balanced with computer science. I loved to learn, and to learn about everything.

Give yourself the same opportunities. Read lots of books. Do lots of experiments and math. Discuss everything, try to understand others' perspectives, learn from those around you. Don't predict your future; explore what you love from all angles. You can, and should, develop broad knowledge, especially "useless" knowledge. This useless knowledge has served me well since then; surprisingly, I have often used concepts from Edmund Burke, or from various theories of how organizations form, in day-to-day interactions. That is the stuff that will add colour to your life and your career in the future. It may not be applied, but such useless knowledge turns out to be very useful.

As you are learning that broad knowledge, be open to surprises. I did not expect to found a company in Southeast Asia, and have a great time teaching people about technology. But I did, and it was a lovely experience. I learned a great deal about culture and communication. I am a better person because of that time. Some of your best learning opportunities will be things you never expected. Perhaps travel will give you a new idea. A random television show might spur a fascinating train of thought. Noting an inconsistency might lead you to a groundbreaking new career – this is how I ended up with a doctorate.

Give yourself the opportunity to get this random benefit. Go take a class you wouldn't take normally. You may want to take it for no credit, but go take a class at which you expect to fail. I took an art history class, and I have absolutely no eye for art. I didn't do well, but I recently had an interesting conversation with a colleague about how art informed the medical sciences of the time.

I very much enjoyed that conversation, and I think I have made a new friend who knows a great deal about my current industry. This brings me to my next theme: Relationships matter more than you think they do. Not simply the relationship with your boyfriend (or girlfriend). That relationship matters. But the people around you, those you like and those you don't get along with – they matter too. When you are 18, it is tempting to dismiss those with whom you do not agree. It's tempting to attack them, to trash them, to generally try to crush them beneath your boot heel.

Don't do it. Life is short, but it is also very long. You don't know when that beetle you crushed will be useful to you. Destroying a relationship is sometimes called burning a bridge. Your future journey may take you over that bridge. If so, I hope you didn't burn it – it's hard to traverse a partially destroyed bridge.

I know, you don't need anyone, so the bridges you burn aren't important. If you are like me, you currently think bridges don't matter; sitting comfortably a few decades later, I assure you, you are wrong in that belief. Being able to rely on others is one of the great comforts we have in this world – even if you don't know it yet. In good times and bad, it's nice to have people around you who are on your side. It's more fun to be able to share your triumphs and your troubles, and know that they will celebrate the first and help overcome the second.

Learn to rely on others. No matter what you do, how smart and how strong you are, eventually a crisis will overcome you, and you will need help. Relying on others does not make you weak; pretending to be an island unto yourself makes you weak. I like to use a loaded term to describe relying on others: "To rely on someone else is to be vulnerable to them." Since relying on others makes you strong, being vulnerable to others, and accepting that vulnerability, makes you strong. Those who admit vulnerability are stronger than those who are unable to do so. The people who are unable to do so are afraid that others will laugh, or treat them badly, or fail to act. Others may, indeed laugh, or be generally unhelpful. But be stronger, better – ask them for help. You never know what will happen. If you are lucky, the support you receive may change your entire life.

Actually, sometimes you will know what will happen. If the people you ask for help are exactly like you, they will likely suggest what you would have suggested to them. Sometimes this is exactly what you need – someone to tell you that your view is right. But often, you need an alternative perspective, a divergent view on the problem. And you won't get this from a clone of yourself. You will only get different views on a problem from people who are, in fact different from you. This is my third theme: Diversity matters. Connect with diverse people, it will help you on your journey. As you form relationships on which you can rely, surround yourself with people from different backgrounds than you. Maybe you need to join a club that's not related to your background, or your direct interests. Maybe you need to eat in a different cafeteria every day, forcing yourself to meet new people. You can always find diversity if you look – go look for it, and make surprising relationships. These relationships will be harder to form, and will often include some conflict as your views clash with each other, but are among the most valuable you will have as you travel your life road.

So that's it. When I was 18, I wish I had known to be open to surprises, and to recognize I couldn't plan my whole life out. I wish I had understood the value of relationships, especially diverse ones. Many of the joys in my life have come from surprises, from friends, and from eagerly looking around that next bend in the journey.

I wish you the same joy. Have fun.

> " You need moral courage, as
> no great things can be achieved without it. "

Lord Paddy Ashdown

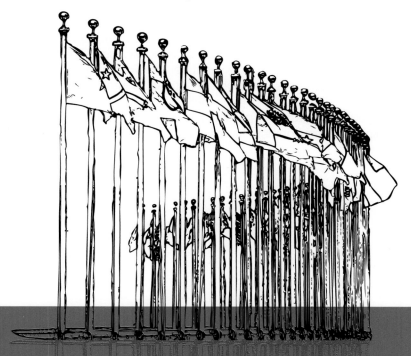

Politics

Politics

The world of politics can be harsh, cruel and confusing at times. However it is an area that remains important in society and is ever-present in the media. Decision making is vital, and therefore it is important have leadership and good communication skills to enter this field.

Many people believe the only career in politics is through parliament however there are many other doors that are open to you. Journalism, political research and the entire civil service are a few of the various other possibilities. Politics is a massive area so it might be a good idea to think what you would like to do and in what kind of environment. Then there is the option of national or international politics.

Whatever you decide to do in politics, it is certainly a rewarding career as your will be operating in an environment that is constantly changing and extremely relevant.

LORD PADDY ASHDOWN

Profession/short job description:
Pretending to be retired after a life of being; a soldier, diplomat, politician, international peace maker and serving in the House of Lords.

How did you make your first steps to success, and what do you consider to be the key to your success?
I do not know the honest answer. My life happened by accident as apposed to by design. I do however remember the biggest and most important decision being the most stupid; I gave up a well paid job in the foreign office to go into politics, whilst I was supporting a family with two children.

It may not have been the best decision at the time but it turned out to be the best. If there is one thing I learnt at school it is that "if ever I am faced with two paths, I always take the more difficult", something which the great John Bunyan once said. So I suppose in this sense, moral courage will lead to success. You need to be a goal driven person.

What have been your most valuable career-defining experiences?
I can not name one in particular, but the best gift I got from my career is being able to assess risks. I find that the problem today is that most people grow up in cotton wool, protected by their parents too much. So they do not grow up with danger, and therefore can not access the risks accurately. To me a crisis is a danger, but also an opportunity.

What do you wish you had known when you were younger?
I wish I had not wasted the opportunity to gain more knowledge. Most of the knowledge I now posses I learnt later on in life. So I was unable to make the best use of this.

Do you have a personal Mantra?
Not as such, but I do believe in plurality which is the belief in that there is more than one basic principle to everything. This is not my mantra for success, but instead my mantra for living.

We are all the more one, because we are many. For we have made an ample space for love in the gap where we were sundered, Our unlikeness reveals its breadth of beauty, with one common life, Like mountain peaks in the morning sun.

Sir Rabindranath Tagore (1861–1941), 'Unity in Diversity' – from his anthology: Oriental Caravan.
Multiplicity is life and nature.

Are there any funny / comic moments that you can remember from your career?
Yes there are too many for me to explain here. Most of the funny incidents have been at my own expense though, unfortunately. If you read my autobiography it will tell you all about those funny moments.

What advice would you have for young people just starting out in the world?
I have no direct advice for young people, as I do not want to sound too pompous. However I will say try to seek adventure, gain experiences while you are still young enough to do so.

Is there anything else that you would like to add?
I am far too wise to tell you what my mistakes were in life. I will add that the greatest human attribute after love of course, is moral courage. This is very hard to find, it is a rarer thing than to find courage on the battle field. You need moral courage, as no great things can be achieved without it.

LORD BIRT

Member of the House of Lords

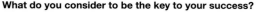

Lord Birt's main career was in broadcasting. He started in programmes at Granada TV and ended up as Director-General of the BBC. After his period in broadcasting, he was Tony Blair's Strategy Adviser at Number 10 from 2000 – 2005. Then he became an adviser to, or a director of, a number of companies in the UK and Europe. Currently he is an adviser to the private equity group Terra Firma, and Chairman of Maltby, EMI's holding company.

What do you consider to be the key to your success?
A lot of luck, mixed in with really heavy-duty analysis of both problems and opportunities, clear goals and a stubborn unwillingness to give up!

What was your most valuable career-defining experience?
Starting a current affairs programme in the 1970s, called Weekend World, and through that meeting and learning from some of the most insightful thinkers in political, economic and foreign affairs.

Do you have a personal mantra?
The motto I chose for my coat of arms was 'Ad Meliora' – towards a better world!

What do you wish you had known when you were younger that you don't know now?
Nothing at all! I wouldn't want to miss the exhilarating adventure of trying it for myself – experimenting and sometimes failing – and learning accordingly. It wouldn't have been so much fun if I had had it right first time!

GORDON BROWN

Prime Minister

At a very young age I became interested in politics. I grew up in the town of Kirkcaldy, an industrial centre, which when I was young was undergoing major change, with rising unemployment and desperate poverty. Both of my parents, John and Elizabeth, were influential figures in my life. My father was not only a Minister of the Church, but also played a central part in town life. I remember my father being very interested in helping people. He often helped those in desperate circumstances who saw the minister's house as their only refuge for help.

I recall my father quoting the words of Martin Luther King: "everyone can be great because everyone can serve". My parents are my inspiration, and the reason I am in politics today. At school and at University I took an interest in political campaigns and enjoyed political debates I also enjoyed my studies and playing sport. After graduating from university I became a college lecturer and wrote several books before becoming MP for Dunfermline East in 1983 with a majority of 11,000.

I was honoured to be asked by Her Majesty The Queen to become the Prime Minister. I really do think it is the best job in the world. This is because I am able to do things every day which help to make the lives of young people better, not just in Britain but also in some of the poorest countries around the world.

Being Prime Minister can be hard work, like many other jobs. It is difficult to tell you what it's like because no single day is the same, and there are a huge range of things to do.

In any single day, for example, I might have meetings with ministers and civil servants to decide what to do about schools, hospitals, the police, the army or other important issues. I might have to answer questions or make a statement in the House of Commons. I might even have meetings with Her Majesty The Queen or with the leaders of other countries who are visiting London. I also regularly spend days out of the office visiting other towns and cities around the country to speak to people there and find out what changes they want to see. Every so often, I go abroad to visit other countries so that we can make international agreements to improve the environment, or to tackle poverty, or to work together to create jobs.

My personal mantra is that every child should have the best start in life, that everybody should have the chance of a job, that nobody should be brought up suffering in poverty. I would call them the beliefs that you associate with civilisation and dignity.

Bedford School 1950- 55.

I was a Senior Monitor, Head of Ashburnham, Head of Chapel Choir, 1st XV Rugby cap, English Schoolboys, 1st IV Fives, 1st VI Tennis, 2nd XI Cricket and Mitre Club. A level English and History Reflections on School. I thoroughly enjoyed school. I was inspired by Masters like Mr Squibs, Owen Bevan and John Eyre although the latter with his Socialist views have much influenced me to become a Conservative.

THOUGHTS:
To get the most out of life one needs to join in with enthusiasm and one makes life long friends providing one's friendships are kept in repair.

National Service 1950-55

I was scheduled to go into the Gunners having been a Sergeant in the Combined Cadet Force (CCF). However I changed my mind having got a Private Pilots licence in the summer whilst visiting my parents in Pakistan. I still remember the Sergeant at the recruiting office in Catford, London saying ' you can't change your mind' I quietly pointed out I could. Resulting in me having to wait all day to be reprocessed but I taken a good book so I was patient. At the assessment at RAF Hornchurch we had to listen to Morse Code and write down when we heard something. The chap on my right started immediately I listened, could not hear anything for about a minute. I was right there was nothing - Lesson stick to your own evidence not what others do. I qualified as a full RAF pilot with Wings.

THOUGHTS: In today's world I would definitely go for a Gap year and travel.

Cambridge - St Catharine's College 1957-60

Originally scheduled to read one years Economics and two years Law. However I got an Upper Second in Economics so decided to stick with the subject. I also graduated with an Upper second. Lesson: stick with what you are good at and don't be afraid to change. I did not enjoy Cambridge as much as school partly because of the experience of National Service. Each student had a supervisor for their academic work and we had to write an essay every two weeks. Two shared a supervision and after writing 4 essays we asked when they would be marked and returned. Professor Berrill said in due time. Neither my colleague nor I were satisfied with this answer so we complained to our tutor who said it was unprecedented to complain but we got all the essays back, properly marked and were given special attention there after.

THOUGHTS: Never be afraid to complain if you are in the right.

Commerce -1960-1974

My first job was with the Reckitt and Colman Group. I had asked to work overseas as I had no money and it was better paid. I worked in India/Ceylon and UK. Great experience on the selling and marketing side and I saved some money. After 5 years I decided I needed Advertising Agency experience. I worked for 3 Agencies initially as a Marketing Executive but very soon switched to Account Handling as that led to the Board. I became a director in 2 of the Agencies. I thoroughly enjoyed these years, worked hard and found I was good at visualisation. I also really looked after my clients and ensured they all made a profit for the Agency

THOUGHTS: Look after clients at every level but insist on making a profit and try to make yourself reasonably financially independent

Politics-1974-

I got the politics bug in Sri Lanka (Ceylon). My best friend was a Sri Lankan, Head of J Walter Thompson Ad Agency and he was going to stand for Parliament. I knew I had a latent idea to right a few wrongs In the World. When I came back to the UK I asked to meet Jim Prior MP who told me what I had to do to try to become an MP. I did my apprenticeship fighting Islington North in 1966 , lost went on the Council in Islington in 1968 thanks to the unpopularity of Harold Wilson, became Leader and then in February 1974 fought Northampton South and won by 1979. I represented the seat until 1997 when the anti Tory tidal wave took me out. I was then asked to go to the House of Lords as a working Peer where I am today asking difficult Questions of the Government. I was never a Minister which I regret but I fear I rebelled too often as I tried to vote as my conscience dictated. However it held me in good stead because when it came to electing the Chairman of Ways and Means /Deputy Speaker I won handsomely with support from all sides of the House because it was recognised I was not a Party hack.

FINAL THOUGHTS:
Apart from those above:

Have a long term strategy.
Don't take 'NO' for an answer.
Learn to ask short penetrating questions.
Never be afraid to cold call.
Learn to read a balance sheet.

HENRY VANN

Liberal Democrat parliamentary
campaigner for Bedford & Kempston

I am the Liberal Democrat parliamentary campaigner for Bedford and Kempston and I am also the youngest Liberal Democrat parliamentary campaigner in the UK.

At Bedford, I had never really thought I was interested in politics, but in my final year, myself and a group of friends wrote a manifesto of what we thought should be done and wondered if we should set up our own party; the Iraq war was fresh in our minds, and plenty of other problems, in our eyes, needed solving.

Of course, what I didn't know until my first year at University was that most of our policies were already policies of the Liberal Democrats.

My advice to anyone reading this would be to go and find out right now what each party stands for, and have a think about what you stand for. It doesn't take long, an on-line search is usually sufficient and this will give you a proper idea of what a party believes.

Of course, it is all but impossible to agree with everything a political party says – but don't let this put you off. Parties can change their policies, and what matters (or perhaps what should matter) is the underlying philosophy of that party.

Whichever university you go to, there will be a real opportunity to try everything. But don't get bogged down in student politics. Politics at university between warring factions can be intimidating, and off-putting. Don't let this get you down, you can join a national party without ever having to deal with this sort of tribalism, or if debating does appeal to you, then give it a go.

One particularly enjoyable moment was returning to speak to the Mitre Club, as a former member, a few months ago. I really enjoyed the questions from students who knew a lot more about the parliamentary system than I did in my final two years at Bedford School.

Politics is open to anyone, so give it a try. If you are unhappy, find yourself frustrated with the way things are run, or have a really good plan to improve where you live, then get involved.

"Never be arrogant, but always be self-confident" was something that was suggested to me as a way to proceed when speaking in public. And remember, people are often cynical about politicians, but speak to any councillor, parliamentarian, or candidate, and they will have a genuine concern for the area they are seeking to represent; the cynicism is often unwarranted.

Within any political group there is usually something summarising the philosophy of that party and the Liberal Democrats are not different. When I need to respond to a political question, I can run it by the party's constitution which states that we "exist to build and safeguard a fair free and open society ... in which no-one shall be enslaved by poverty, ignorance, or conformity."

> To be No 1
> you have to train like you're No 2

Lawrence Dallaglio

Sport

Sport

As with the world of music, sport is an extremely challenging area in which to secure professional status. Whether you become a P.E. teacher or a professional rugby player, dedication is essential. Long hours will be required but if this isn't something you fancy, there is always the option of going into something less physically demanding such as commentating or physiotherapy. How about becoming a stunt performer?

Obviously physical fitness is essential as well as good communication skills. Whatever sport you take up, you will be seen as a professional and therefore a role model to others and following the rules will be crucial.

RODDY CAXTON-SPENCER

Extreme Adventurer

'In the Arctic, as in life, you dance with the Devil. You have to watch and respect his every move, because if you don't he will strike hard and fast and it will hurt like Hell'.

It can feel unpleasant and somewhat risky to challenge your own world, but then if you do nothing about it what have you really achieved! You will regret in times to come the chances you did not take, the initiative you did not show and what you dreamt about but didn't do. One of the problems is that if you tell yourself a challenge is impossible, and I tell you are wrong, we could both be right. Amudson once wrote 'Victory awaits those who have everything in order—People call that luck—Defeat is certain for those who have forgotten to take the necessary precautions and time---That is called bad luck'.

In my honest opinion when I am climbing a mountain or walking across the arctic, I believe my day has probably been decided before I leave my tent. I don't know when I first started to think that anything may be possible. At several points in my life, I certainly felt that I had reached my limit.

I lived my dreams when both asleep and awake. I dreamed of climbing high mountains, sailing across oceans, or following in the footsteps of an explorer or two. The problem was that I used to think that what one dreamed about was so achievable, but not by me. It took a quantum leap of faith in my own self belief to realise that the dream is not simply a mental state, but is also a genuine realisable ambition. Today I would advise anyone to put away what you believe to be your own limitations; your own personal expectations can be raised beyond your wildest dreams no matter what they are.

I was recently asked 'What is your next challenge' I replied 'To learn how to play the saxophone' 'Is that all', came the response, but to me that was the biggest challenge I could have set myself. It is not all about climbing mountains or walking across deserts, it's about setting your own targets outside your comfort zone, and believing you can achieve them. How do we realistically realise these dreams and ambitions? The possibilities increase as we grow up but the will to reach beyond ourselves tends to diminish. Our dreams then grow fewer and more inhibited.

The lesson is to try to grow into the person you really want to become.

LAWRENCE DALLAGLIO

Professional International Rugby Player

Profession/short job description:
Professional Rugby Player for London Wasps/England/British Lions from 1989-2008. Now a Director on the Board at London Wasps.

How did you make your first steps to success, and what do you consider to be the key to your success?
There's no one answer to this question and it's normally always a combination of things! I had a good support base from my upbringing! My parents taught me manners and an appreciation of certain values in life. Values that hopefully carry you through to the rest of your life. Values that are relevant to success irrespective of your chosen career!
Hard work, honesty, integrity, a Winning mentality. Desire, Excellence, Pride and Loyalty.
Success to me means rich with life.
Success means being a winner!
Success to me means not settling for mediocrity.
Success means making your niche in History.

What have been your most valuable career-defining experiences?
We are what we are exposed to in life. Good and bad. To appreciate the best you have to experience the worst. Adversity brings out the best in all of us. We take the positives from any situation. Learn the lessons and move forward to become better off.

Career defining experiences for me would be:
Losing my sister in The Marchioness Riverboat disaster in 1989.
Missing out on selection for England Schools team at under 18 level.
Winning the world cup 7s in 1993 with England.
Knee injury ACL in 2001
Ankle fracture/dislocation in 2005 on Lions Tour.

What do you wish you had known when you were younger
My Mum's mother!

Do you have a personal Mantra?
To be No 1 you have to train like you're No 2

Are there any funny / comic moments that you can remember from your career?
So many to mention. Most of them involving my good pal Jason Leonard or Jerry Guscott.
The first England match I played pre professional rugby was against France in Paris. I was rooming with Ben Clarke. Two days before the match all the lads came round to our room in the hotel and polished off about 10 bottles of red wine.

The next morning Ben Clarke ordered me to go and hide the empties around the corner. I was walking down the corridor in my dressing gown carrying a tray of empty wine bottles and bumped straight into Jack Rowell- England Head Coach. That wasn't very funny!!!

What advice would you have for young people just starting out in the world of?
Be humble and work hard. Any successful person has to be prepared to suffer to achieve that success.

Is there anything else that you would like to add?
Successful teams are characterized by:

- Good leadership and are well managed
- They design for the future
- They have engaged and motivated people
- They put the right people in the right roles.
- They have a team agenda, not a personal agenda
- They show spirit and cheerfulness in adversity.

Photo: www.richardlanephotography.co.uk

BRIAN DISBURY

English Cricketer

Job Description

From the age of 7, I was preoccupied with playing cricket to the detriment of any scholastic achievements. My 2 years of National Service in the RAF were spent playing sports – rugby, tennis, squash and cricket at station level but the summers were spent playing cricket, in the RAF side and in a Combined Service side against the Public School's team at Lords.

I did not get a university degree nor did I pass my Chartered Accountancy examinations while playing cricket for Kent 1954 –58. However, my accounting experience proved useful when I replied to an advert by Anglo American of Johannesburg, for Accountants in Zambia in 1966.I was hired as an accountant, I suspect, not because of my qualifications but because I had played for Kent against Jack Cheetham's South African Touring side.

After a brief stay in Bancroft as an Auditor I was transferred to Broken Hill in Kabwe were I was in charge of the Mines metal sales (Lead, Zinc, Gold and Silver) throughout Africa. I was later transferred to the London Office in 1972 where I had the responsibility for the International sales of all metals, and was an advisor to the Tugsten Commodity Committee of UNCTAD in Geneva. Finally, I was a director of Anmersales, a branch of Anglo, during the oil recession in the mid 70's, a time of high inflation and high mortgage interest while on fixed salaries. In 1977 I accepted a post with Hudson Bay Mining in Toronto as an assistant manager at three times the salary.

After a spell in New York and Phoenix Arizona with the I.C.C.C, another Anglo subsidiary, I retired from Anglo in 1987,but this was short lived as Cyprus Minerals invited me to join them in Denver. After 3 years I accepted a position with Magma Copper Company as Vice President- Commercial, being responsible for the International purchase of the Raw materials and the sale of finished products. I retired in August 1996.

Over my 30 years in the mining industry from 1966-1996, I made many friends, met a lot of high- powered executives and had a wonderful time. On reflection, the whole of my mining career, apart from my initial response to the Anglo advert, was by invitation. The metal market had a limited number of successful Marketing / Sales people and not having a University Degree I could never be a Board member. I was therefore no threat to my Boss and was very well rewarded for my expertise to retain my services. The secret for continuous employment seems to be - becoming an expert in a small and highly specialized field.

The Key to my Success

I had a passion for cricket which lead to Accountancy, after which I followed Yogi Bear's Advice "When you come to a Fork in the road take it". Life always offers opportunities even in disastrous times. My wife and I had 3 young children when we went to Zambia and I had to borrow 50 pounds to get us to Heathrow. We never looked back and had a great time there. Never pass up an opportunity you never know where it might lead you…learn from the experience whatever the circumstances.

My most career-defining experiences

My career was full of them, but the first one set the standard for me to be a trader. It was my first day in the London office from Zambia and I had just concluded my first sale to a director of the largest international metal trading company in London, on the phone. As a very smug Brian was sitting back in his chair, cogitating on telling his boss of his great deal, the phone rang - it was the person that I had concluded the business with. He asked me if I was happy about the deal and I told him yes. He then explained that he wanted to have a long term business relationship with me and I would probably get fired when I told my President of our deal. He proceeded to restate the terms of the contract which were much more beneficial to me. I was lucky and determined to be a better trader/salesman. Also that I should never take advantage of the lack of expertise of any buyer when I became an expert. Negotiations, thereafter became fun.

What do I wish that I had known when I was younger?

The simple answer is "Everything that I know now!!!".However, as that is not possible, it is to have an open mind- listen to advice given but question whether it sounds true. Listen to that inner voice- your intuition, and pay no attention to your ego. Difficult, but the sooner one learns that, the easier life becomes. Think before you speak, don't react, that is your ego and no apology can eliminate detrimental words spoken. As Shakespeare said," Nothing is right or wrong, but thinking makes it so."

My Mantra (Affirmations)

I accept full responsibility for everything that I do and say. "What goes around comes around"- From Yogananda-"GOD's Power is limitless and as I am created in HIS image I have the Strength to overcome all difficulties".

From Krishnamurti, " I don't mind what happens-Life is only an experience"

Funny moments in my career:

I can think of many that were funny- to others but not to me….Example---

I had been invited, by the Bolivian Ambassador, to accompany him to Beijing to discuss business with Comtrade, the Government trading organization in 1973.At a formal dinner one evening I had to suffer my first experience of using round ivory chop sticks, there was not a fork or spoon in sight--the Chinese hosts were highly amused by my antics. Their President, spoke to me first in Portuguese and then in very good English. He apologized for speaking Portuguese but as I was representing their Government at Unctad, he assumed that I spoke the language. When he noticed the puzzled look on my face he realized that I was English, as we were renowned for not speaking foreign languages. I then stupidly asked him where he learned Portuguese, to which he replied, " In a Brazilian jail". He was grateful for the conversation in that he had saved money as the Bolivian Ambassador and I could go in the same car the next day to view the Great Wall and the Forbidden City as we only need one Interpreter.

What advice would I give a young person starting out in cricket?

Practice, Practice, Practice. When I was 12 and my sister was 8, I used to get her to throw a golf ball at me on wet concrete (as it slipped though faster), and I had to play it back to her with a cricket stump. I also spent a lot of time in front of a full- length mirror playing strokes to make sure that I picked the bat up straight. As we practiced (my sister was batting with the stump), it became obvious that she had a better eye for the ball than I did-we practiced for hours.(She later went on tour to Australia/New Zealand with Rachel Hehoe's English Test team.).

When I played cricket in Zambia I had started to wear glasses and could see the ball much better for catching and it helped my batting too. I realized that I had managed to play to a reasonable standard of cricket in England, even though my eyesight was not great, my reflexes were slow, I was not a fast runner and did not exactly have a Mr World physique.

Anyone who has the physical attributes, more importantly, a passion for playing cricket, can be trained to play first class cricket, with a lot of hard work, dedication to success, accepting failures as part of the learning process, make all things possible. Ask those who have, or are still playing Test cricket.

I am very grateful for the happy times that I spent playing the Game.

SIR ALEX FERGUSON CBE

Manager of Manchester United Football Club

1) There are certain disciplines one should stick by and in my case they have never changed.

   a) Time keeping, make sure you are up early in the morning ready to attack the whole day, it is amazing how refreshing it is to be up early.
   b) Don't change your beliefs, stick by this principle and in effect you stay true to yourself.

2) When you are young whether 18 or not, don't miss opportunities. I had the opportunity to be a full time footballer at 16 but my Father insisted I had to serve an apprenticeship as an engineer. Now that apprenticeship was a fantastic experience but knowing my real ambition was to be a footballer I often wondered how good I would have been if I had taken the opportunity to go full time. As it turned out I completed my apprenticeship as a toolmaker, served an extra year as a tradesman and then pursued my career as a full time professional at Dunfermline Athletic FC by which time I was almost 23, so those missing 5 years or so that I could have used as a full time pro were lost to me. At that point I made my first steps to stay in football for the remainder of my career and made it my target to become a Manager. Unlike a lot of footballers who finish playing one day and become managers the next I started to take my coaching badges at 24 and had my full coaching certificate at 25. I made sure I was prepared if the opportunity came along to stay in the game once I had finished. As the saying goes, "if you fail to prepare you prepare to fail". When I went into Football Management I was only 32 which was very young but I had prepared for that day and it was a help. One thing I quickly picked up which is always something I had in me was the ability to make decisions quickly and positively; this transmits itself throughout the work force.

ANDY GOMARSALL

Professional Rugby Union Player

Profession/short job description:
I am a professional Rugby Union player. I have played for England and hope to play again for my country before I retire from the game. Once I retire I would like to go into sports or coaching management, I have not totally decided yet; but definitely something to do with sport.

How did you make your first steps to success, and what do you consider to be the key to your success?
Good question. I suppose hard work and dedication. Constant evaluation and reviewing of oneself, to get better with every opportunity.

What have been your most valuable career-defining experiences?
For me going to the World Cup in 1995 and just being there in the atmosphere and being part of the team, even though I didn't get to play. Then winning my first cap, it all turned professional at this point. From nearly losing it all to winning the Rugby World Cup in 2003; this was a very defining moment in my career.

What do you wish you had known when you were younger?
There are a lot of things. But the main one would be the art of negotiation with differing personalities. I wish I had studied the world of politics. When I was at school I had no idea how much politics had an influence over sport.

I wish I had also had an opportunity to be introduced to sport physiology when I was younger, as this is a very important area in the sporting world.

Do you have a personal Mantra?
"To be the best". There have been times when I have not been my best, but it about working to that goal; to get the best out of oneself. Sport is a very competitive area; I was very competitive as a youngster, so I have always wanted to win.

Are there any funny / comic moments that you can remember from your career?
Of course, but some are too graphic to go in here. Laughing about oneself is always good. I am now 'old' in the world of rugby, and so when I look back there always seem to be many dodgy photos of me with public school hair cuts – rather embarrassing.

Being knocked out by the touch judge in 2007 was rather embarrassing.

The England Rugby squad are just a great group of people; they have a great humour off the pitch, but when on the pitch they are serious and focused.

What advice would you have for young people just starting out in the world of sport?
If you want to be the best and number one, you first of all have to have the raw materials and have the skills. You need to keep practising; otherwise your talent will suffer. You have to keep working, you can not afford to be lazy at any stage, you will be found out. Keep the basics and home them in, this will help you be the best. The physiology of sport is important, so be mentally tough. This is why England can do well in the World Cup; as they are mentally tough. It can be coached and practised, you can train yourself to be mentally fit.

You need skill and mental toughness, but when you are young you do not understand until you are at the top level.

GARY LEWIN
Msc GradDipPhys MCSP SRP MSC

Head of Physiotherapy - England
Senior Men's Football Team

I wish that I had known more about peoples cultures, history and religion when I was 18. In today's multi-cultural world it is essential that people understand and communicate with each other.

"A World Class Organisation with a Winning Mentality"

DAME ELLEN MACARTHUR

Offshore sailor and communicator

Th. Martinez/Sea&Co/
BT Team Ellen

How did you make your first steps to success, and what do you consider to be the key to your success?
I was just four when I stepped onto a boat for the very first time, and it was a moment that changed my life forever. I loved every minute of it, the feeling of total freedom and that I had the ability to sail anywhere in this tiny boat was amazing to me. From then on I was hooked and read every book about sailing that I could get my hands on. Sailing undoubtedly became a passion for me and I would spend every opportunity I had on the water or in the boat yard working on every boat that I could get my hands on. I am still inspired every time I get out on the water; sailing is a great sport in the sense that each experience can be a new one and you can always learn a new skill, even after years of being out on the water.

My Nan was a real inspiration to me - she got her degree at the age of 83! - and she taught me some important lessons which have been hugely helpful both throughout my career and in life generally: to show courage, determination and never give up. I think those words ringing in my ears have pushed me to carry on during difficult moments at sea.

What have been your most valuable career-defining experiences?
The Southern Ocean is unique. Never in my life before have I experienced such beauty, and fear at the same time. It wants everything. When you have nothing left, it wants twice as much again. It taught me to dig deep into reserves that I didn't know I had.

What do you wish you had known when you were younger?
To not take life too seriously and remember to have fun!

Do you have a personal Mantra?
"A donf!" - an expression I learnt when I was working in a boatyard in France. It translates as "Go for it!"

Are there any funny / comic moments that you can remember from your career?
Absolutely loads! My funniest experience sailing was doing the Transat Jacques Vabre in 200X with a French sailor called Roland Jourdain who is more commonly known by his nickname 'Bilou'. I don't think I have every laughed so much on a boat. At one point, we were going through really rough seas. The boat suddenly pitched and Bilou did an unintentional somersault - for about 15 minutes after that we were helpless with laughter!

What advice would you have for young people just starting out in the world?
Follow your own path and never stop questioning and learning.

Is there anything else that you would like to add?
Life can get very busy and it is easy to lose touch with what really matters - take time to appreciate all the precious things in life.

CHRISTOPH METZELDER

Professional Football Player, Real Madrid

In May 2000, I signed my first professional contract with Borussia Dortmund. At that time, I was 19 and right in the middle of my "abitur" (A-Level exams). It was obviously not the easiest step to change from "Preußen Münster", in the third league, to one of the most ambitious teams in Germany at that point. However, it shows the key to my personal success: ambition, and to set oneself the highest targets possible. This, combined with discipline and a keen perception helped me quickly learn how the football business works and how to reach the "Bundesliga" (Premiership) level.

Every event that influences your life has got to do with people. In my career, but also in other areas, I was lucky that I knew people who knew my potential. Mathias Sammer, coach of Borussia Dortmund, Rudi Völler or Jürgen Klinsmann the Germany coach – they all believed in me and my strengths, "invested" in me and therefore I had the confidence to pay them back.

I am not a guy who looks back at the past. I made all my decisions after informing myself and having talked to people I trusted and who were important to me. Unfortunately, in Germany there is not the mentality to see injuries as a normal part of a professional's life, after having suffered from a setback. However, I have always understood this "learning process" to adapt myself to a professional's life in Germany.

"The bigger the obstacle you have overcome, the bigger the victory".

As a sportsman, one loves to think back to victories and titles, but I think, what you cannot ever forget are the people who have been through the same kind of things like you. There are lots and lots of funny anecdotes, sentences, which connect you to others. Even years later. What I really like to remember is a journey to a "Karneval" feast in Cologne. We traveled there in a BVB (Borussia Dortmund) – Team bus, dressed up as pilots. This was one of the funniest moments in my career.

I am convinced that every human has got extraordinary abilities. Whether in sport, music, literature or working with children and the ill. The important thing is, to discover one's own passions and to follow them insistently. The crucial thing is that adults have got the responsibilities to transmit the maximum of attention, respect and motivation to all young people in order for them to find the right way of life. To support this, I established the "Christoph-Metzelder-Stiftung" (Christoph - Metzelder Trust). This trust supports education and other important projects in Germany.

It might sound very precocious, but you are NOW in the time in which you lay the fundaments for your life. Of course it is important, to enjoy youth, jokes and try many different things. Everyone should enjoy those; but I know too many people who look back at 30 and say: "If earlier I had … then today I would be…"

BUDGE ROGERS OBE

Ex- England Rugby Captain & Businessman

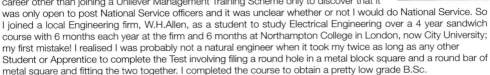

A chequered career leading to success

I left Bedford School in 1957 with A-Levels in Mathematics and Physics and no idea of a career other than joining a Unilever Management Training Scheme only to discover that it was only open to post National Service officers and it was unclear whether or not I would do National Service. So I joined a local Engineering firm, W.H.Allen, as a student to study Electrical Engineering over a 4 year sandwich course with 6 months each year at the firm and 6 months at Northampton College in London, now City University; my first mistake! I realised I was probably not a natural engineer when it took my twice as long as any other Student or Apprentice to complete the Test involving filing a round hole in a metal block square and a round bar of metal square and fitting the two together. I completed the course to obtain a pretty low grade B.Sc.

The next few years presented me with a problem of balancing playing rugby with work, all be it as an amateur, for Bedford and England ,hence I rather jumped from job to job with no clear plan other than to gain sales and management experience which I did particularly with a Canadian direct sale Life Assurance company and P.A. Management Consultants.

It was not until I joined C.T. Bowring as my rugby career ended to open a new insurance broking office for them in the emerging town of Milton Keynes, that I found my niche. A role using my natural selling skills as well as management skills and offering a real challenge. Interestingly I knew practically nothing about general insurance but did understand business and could talk about the needs for insurance and service to potential customers. I recall so well the excitement among the small team when we were appointed by our first commercial client. After building this office I became Managing Director of a much bigger branch in Manchester where I carried out a major restructuring of the business and turned a loss into profit. After two other positions of Chief Executive of London insurance brokers in 1991 I purchased a broker in Rickmansworth, moved it to Milton Keynes and grew it by organic growth and acquisitions until selling it in 2003.

I believe that key factors in my business success were:

- Good interpersonal skills with staff and clients
- Seeing the big picture without losing sight of the detail
- Engendering in my business the vital importance of client service
- A real understanding of the financial elements of business
- Good selling and networking skills
- Setting a good example to staff

Looking back there are a number of lessons I have learnt or things I would have done differently:

- To have gone into insurance broking much earlier
- To have started my own business much earlier
- To have been bolder in my business by borrowing more to acquire more

It would have been difficult to predict that this was the right career for me, so in setting your sights on a career, unless you have a long term clear view , consider the following:

- Take GCE's and a degree you are going to enjoy
- Talk to as many people about the industry/ profession as possible and try to get into firms to see how they operate
- Try to imagine the roles to which your style and personality would be suited
- Remember that employers place as high a price on commitment, honesty reliability and how you will fit into their organisation as ability as expressed by success in exams.

I mentioned earlier that in my early working years my involvement in Rugby was a major draw on my time and rather more important than my career. I have been asked to give some guidance on a "career in sport". I think this is a more difficult decision than choosing a business career. I say this for two reasons; firstly, to reach the very top in a sport is extremely difficult and requires not only ability and application but also a large slice of luck i.e. who else around, right place at right time ,selection etc. Secondly a career in sport is so susceptible to injury.

With the glamour and high earnings attached to the major professional sports you will, if good , be under pressure often from your parents and certainly from the sporting body who in its own thirst for success will encourage many more young players to join them than they can eventually utilize at the top. So, be careful and try to be very self-analytical and critical of your ability and application in assessing your real chance of success and, if you do embark on a full-time sporting career, insist that in the early years you continue some tertiary education and plan for an alternative career because for a variety of reasons you might at 25/26 need to do something else. I was lucky, I could play at the highest level and still have a career.

> I have seen whales and swum with manta rays, and know more about the guts of barnacles than any person alive.

Professor Phil Rainbow

Zoology

Zoology

A zoologist is an expert in the field of zoology - the study of animals. Your work could vary considerably from researching animal behaviour to feeding them in their natural habitat. Most zoologists will specialise in one group or species of animals although some will go into other areas such as palaeontology (study of ancient environments) or ethology (study of animal behaviour) where they will be dealing with many different groups.

There is an opportunity to work abroad as you may be involved with the conducting of scientific identification and the recording of a huge range of animal species in their natural habitats. The world's your oyster.

A genuine interest in animals, a logical mind and good organisation skills are all desirable when considering zoology as a career however competition for jobs is tough and employers looking for a zoologist like to see some volunteer work done beforehand in museums or other establishments that are relevant to zoology as it helps you to become familiar with data recording techniques and other skills essential to any zoologist.

PROFESSOR PAUL HARVEY CBE

My name is Paul Harvey. I'm a Professor at the University of Oxford where, for the last ten years I have been Head of the Department of Zoology. Eight years ago I took over as Secretary of the Zoological Society of London (ZSL), so I'm responsible for London Zoo, Whipsnade Zoo, the Society's Research Institute, and Conservation projects in over 80 countries. I get expenses but don't get paid for the ZSL work, which I do for fun.

I'm a product of the state school system. This was the days of the 11+, which I passed (my sister who was as bright as me failed, which shows the iniquity of the process). I went to a small, local grammar school in Worcestershire. I was either bottom of my class or second from bottom for the first three years. I loved country walks, usually alone, and did a lot of fishing. In our fourth year, a new biology teacher arrived and he explained about evolution – that was it as far as I was concerned. What a unifying idea to make sense of natural history! I took my GCE in biology a year early and passed. I also started working well at other subjects. The biology teacher left, so much of my A level biology was self-taught.

Academically, I had excelled in Chemistry in my final year at school but concluded it was boring because once you know the periodic table of the elements everything else follows. Biology would be more interesting. I went to York University as part of the first intake of Biology undergraduates. That was a fantastic experience because all of the faculty were in place to teach three years' worth of students, so we got very individual attention. I stayed on to do research on the evolution of snails for my doctorate.

Although I had never been taught marine biology (and I was raised in the midlands far from the sea) I went straight into a lectureship in marine biology at Swansea – I guess that understanding the principles of evolution means that you can quickly pick up anything biological. My wife, who I had met as a student at York, also got a job at Swansea, but suggested we move to Sussex where evolution was more the core of research in the Department. I got a job there and spent about 13 years building a research group that used evolutionary theory to reveal patterns of repeated change encompassing many groups of animals from monkeys to birds. I got quite a name for myself and we spent years and terms researching and teaching in the States, including Harvard, Princeton and Seattle. Our two sons were born in Harvard and Seattle during my wife's maternity leave, which is when it was easiest for us to get away.

In 1984 it was suggested that I apply for a job at Oxford, which I did, and I've been in the same office ever since though the job has changed. I started as a lecturer, became a reader, then a Professor and was elected as a Fellow of the Royal Society. But those are just names – it was building and maintaining an active research group, always asking new questions that was satisfying. Also, teaching the evolution course with Richard Dawkins was an experience I would not have missed. Then things really did change: I was made Head of Department. That meant working for your colleagues rather than following your own agenda. It has been a pleasure to develop and realise a vision of how a Department should evolve.

In my experience, it is important to have diverse influences and experiences. To that end, I have worked on grant giving bodies and on various Royal Society committees over the years. But I needed something more substantial, and the offer of the job as Secretary of ZSL provided that. With my colleagues, I've helped the society to realise a new vision embodied in our new motto: Living Conservation. Our field conservation programmes have increased enormously in scope, magnitude and relevance. At the same time our Zoo animals are increasingly housed as breeding groups in new large enclosures – each year, fewer species are found in cages. The Department of Zoology now researches animal welfare, while the Zoos implement it.

PROF PHIL RAINBOW

Keeper of Zoology, The Natural History Museum, London

The title 'Keeper of Zoology' at the Natural History Museum dates back to the formation of the Department of Zoology in 1856, although the first Keeper of the Zoological Branch of the Natural History Department of the British Museum was appointed in 1837, and the first Keeper of the wider Natural Department dates from 1756. The position is therefore one steeped in history. Translated today, the position is that of the Head of Department of Zoology at the Natural History Museum, so familiar to many at South Kensington in London. What is probably less familiar is that the Department of Zoology is the largest of five research departments behind the scenes at the Natural History Museum, the others being the Departments of Botany, Entomology, Mineralogy and Palaeontology. Of course entomology (the study of insects) should be part of zoology (the study of animals), but this department was hived off in 1913 given the enormous numbers of insects in the zoological collections.

And so to numbers. The Natural History Museum holds about 70 million specimens for the benefit of scientists throughout the world. The Department of Zoology houses about 29 million of these, ahead of Entomology (28 million), Palaeontology (8 million), Botany (5 million) and Mineralogy (370,000). In addition to 24 curators maintaining and developing the collections, the Department of Zoology has 23 researchers carrying out original research on the taxonomy, systematics, evolution and biodiversity of animals and microbes, while the remainder of the 70 departmental staff supply administrative, consultancy and research support. The nearest equivalent to my role is that of the head of a university department, swapping the students for the specimens. I also play a role in the management and leadership of the Museum in general, interacting with both scientific and non-scientific colleagues.

What am I and how did I get here? I am of course a zoologist but would be better described as a marine biologist. I went to university in 1969 with A levels in zoology, chemistry and physics, really with a view to becoming a biochemist, an exciting new field opening up greatly at the time. I did my share of chemistry and biochemistry, and even enjoyed it, but disillusion set in with Schrodinger's Equation and a requirement to learn the Krebs cycle by rote for examinations. I was fascinated by the biology (natural history?) of animals, particularly by marine biology, and was able to make the choice to graduate as a zoologist. Furthermore I jumped at the chance to read for a PhD in marine biology, specifically on those fascinating creatures – barnacles. I was still young and could start a real career later. My luck held and after three years I was appointed to a lectureship in the University of London, where I stayed for more than twenty years as lecturer, reader, and then professor and head of department before moving to the NHM.

Would I or could I do it again? I was certainly lucky to be in the right place at the right time to be appointed to positions in which I have found great academic satisfaction, with the opportunity to carry out original research in a field of great interest to me. Did I sacrifice anything? Yes indeed. There was, and indeed still is, little financial reward in a biological research career unless you are one of a small minority whose work can be exploited commercially. Then the rewards are immense. The salaries of university teachers and researchers in the 1970s, 80s and 90s were pathetically low, and I looked with envy at colleagues who had taken a more practical approach to earning a decent wage ahead of academic satisfaction. Of course, it has all paid off now, but knowing what I know now, I would perhaps still choose to become an accountant or enter the city. And I write this as the credit crunch is biting hard. So maybe not.

How can I advise would-be zoologists? Firstly do not specialise too early. Choose a university that gives you a good grounding across biology, including biochemistry, molecular biology, genetics and microbiology, and specialise later if you want to go on. A first degree in biological sciences will not over commit you. You should emerge numerate and literate, and in a position to choose whether to stay in biology with little prospect of a huge salary, or whether you want to get a proper job. A Masters course will give you a specialist qualification in a particular biological area if you know now that you want to go that route, but to be an original researcher you will need a PhD – a commitment to three to four years of relative poverty with no guarantee of employment. Only do it if you are not going to resent not being offered a job, and are willing to put down the experience to a period of self development from which you can go into a new career before you are too old. Be prepared to work abroad. By all means go for your dream, but do not become disillusioned and bitter when doors do not open for you.

If you have not been put off yet, what choices should you now consider? To be successful as an independent researcher, you will need to be appointed to a research or university position, and then obtain external grant funding to support your research and build up a team of postgraduate students and postdoctoral researchers around you. You need, therefore, to think ahead in deciding which research skills you will need and what is the research area in which you should like to specialise. Be pragmatic. Think what are the leading research questions of today (or preferably tomorrow) that will attract interest and funding. No-one will pay me to study barnacles for the sake of it, but the environmental consequences of invasive species promoted by climate change may stand a better chance of grant success. Learn modern techniques. Genomic techniques are in vogue at the moment, and many molecular biologists are now turning to whole organism and environmental biologists for advice on the relevant questions to be answered.

So – if you still want to be a zoologist, go for it but don't get bitter. You will not make money and you may have to bale out to pay the bills. I was lucky. I am not rich but, more than 35 years after graduating, I can look back on a career that has given me great satisfaction. I have had the joy of interacting with undergraduates, postgraduates and with scientific collaborators all over the world. I have travelled widely and carried out marine biological research on coral reefs and at the end of Hong Kong sewage pipes. I have seen whales and swum with manta rays, and know more about the guts of barnacles than any person alive. Certainly a rich and varied career, but, in the words of my family, also 'how sad'.

index:

Be part of a successful European social project!

✓ personal
✓ social
✓ safe
✓ competent
✓ professiona

SOPHIA won the international **ACCESS-IT Award 2008** in London. The jury were impressed by the uniqueness of the project, insofar as the company had recognised the needs of elderly people and were able to combine this with innovative technology to improve their quality of life.

Would you like to be our partner for the project in UK?

If you are interested, please contact us via our website:
www.sophia-holding.com

EVENTS   MEDIA   PRINT   DESIGN   PROMOTIONS

Resource Management Design Limited

RESOURCE anything printed, MANAGE all aspects of the project, DESIGN innovative and fresh.

With the government urging businesses to develop and innovate this year, 2009 could turn out to be a great year for those who take up the challenge to be inventive. Difficult economic times mean one thing for certain: change. Now is the time to remain positive and optimistic for the future, look at this as an opportunity, look at what it is you do and how can you improve, and if needed change.

At RMD our inventive team have built a new online system to support our existing clients with the ability to order, review, control and manage all the product they buy from us; this system has been built by our in house web tech's who work with each of our clients to give them what they ask for, each secure login takes the customer to their own bespoke system tailored for their needs. This is a free service and is available to all, logging on through our website clients can see lists, images and history of all the work they place with us. The benefits are many and we would be pleased to demonstrate the system to you, change can be for the better, and the system works for any size of business.

Now more than ever all businesses are reviewing their costs, and an often over looked area is the spend on " Stationery" which includes all printed matter for your business, a core integral part of running your business, Letterheads, business cards, invoices, purchase order books etc, in some instances often left to a more junior member of staff to reorder, without any thought to price. You can benefit from our expertise, allow us the opportunity to audit your spend and we guarantee to save you money, and compromise to service and quality. If you would like to put us to the test please drop an email to laura@rmdl.co.uk and Laura will arrange for our sales director to contact you, let us show how we can save you £££'s on your print and design spend 30 minutes of your time is all the investment you will be asked to make.

It's going to be challenging, but together we can have a successful year.

Gerard Smith
Sales Director

t: 0845 230 4055
w: www.rmdl.co.uk

acknowledgements:

acknowledgements:

Of course we are most grateful to those who have submitted articles for the book. However, we must not only say a thank you to them, but also to those who have helped us produce this book. We are most grateful to each and every one of them for their valuable support.

Thank you:

Mary Ambler
Ann Ayres
John Ayres
Simon Ayres
Colin Baker
Kate Burgess
Michael Cassell
Lillian Connett
Rachel Curtis
Jemmie Elson
Wei Xiang Fan
Katie Green
Peter Green
Dara Grogan
Lesley Harrison
Jill Hammerele
Shaulyn Jackson

Dominique Jenkins
Mechele Kitching
Ashley Knight
Richard Lane
Tom Latchford
Joanne Lock
Mary Richards
John Richards
Brenda Roberts
Gerard Smith
Lesley Stanford
Jeff Stanford
Jamie Tann
Miranda Thomas
Pam Toseland
Gina Worboys

… and finally The Bell Room Staff

corporate
acknowledgements:

acknowledgements:

A thank you to our partners who have helped us along the way to produce the book.

Banner Batteries
www.bannerbatterien.com

Bedford Battery
www.bedfordbattery.co.uk

Bedford School
www.bedfordschool.org.uk

Causeway Technologies
www.causeway.com

CCC Inspirations
www.cccinspirations.com

RMD
www.rmdl.co.uk

Silver
www.silver-worldwide.com

Sophia Holding
www.sophia-holding.com

Waitrose
www.waitrose.com

YouDoDoll
www.youdoodoll.co.uk

Bedford Battery

Co. Ltd

www.bedfordbattery.co.uk

E : info@kiwwih.co.uk
W: www.kiwwih.co.uk
W: www.whatiwishihadknown.co.uk

The Original a21 team

The Original a21 team

Matthew Ayres	Managing Director
Andrew Black	Company Secretary
Wan Shun Fan	Financial Director
Naphat Chittasenee	Technology Director
Sam Jackson	Marketing Director
Phil Salvesen	Sales Director
Ryan Tanna	Operation Director
Ronald Wichhart	Human Resources Director

Kevin Bae
Justin Chan
Maximilian Dyck
Saif Empaya
Ilias Fanteev
Derek Gao
Hayden Green
Theo Green
Kapil Katechia
Callum MacFarlane
Matthew McKeown
Philipp Man
Bernard Ng
Victor Petzinka
Oliver Thomas
Charles Tsai